# A BRIEF HISTORY OF CENTRAL
# AMERICA

# A BRIEF HISTORY
# OF CENTRAL
# AMERICA

### HECTOR PEREZ-BRIGNOLI

Translated by Ricardo B. Sawrey A.
and Susana Stettri de Sawrey

**University of California Press**
*Berkeley · Los Angeles · Oxford*

University of California Press
Berkeley and Los Angeles, California

University of California Press, Ltd.
Oxford, England

Copyright © 1989 by Hector Perez-Brignoli
First published in Spanish by Alianza Editorial,
S.A., © 1985, Madrid.

**Library of Congress Cataloging in Publication Data**
Pérez-Brignoli, Héctor.
[Breve historia de Centroamérica.    English]
A brief history of Central America/Héctor Pérez
Brignoli: translated by Ricardo B. Sawrey A. and
Susana Stetri de Sawrey, p. cm.
Translation of : Breve historia de Centroamérica.
Bibliography: p.
Includes Index.
ISBN 0-520-06049-0 (cloth, alk. paper)
ISBN 0-520-06832-7 (pbk, alk. paper)
  1. Central America—History.  I. Title.
F1436.P4613        1989        972.8        89-31889

Printed in the United States of America

1   2   3   4   5   6   7   8   9

*Forever to Yolanda*

# Contents

# Preface to the Second Edition

In this second edition, appearing now for the first time in English translation, the text has been considerably expanded and revised. Once again, I should like to thank Carolyn Hall and Nicolás Sánchez Albornoz for their comments as well as the readers at the University of California Press. The first edition was well received both in Central America and elsewhere. I would like to repeat two things that I consider important. Because of its brevity, the text can be interpreted in several ways. In other words, I believe that it says more than may seem. Conciseness is not the same as simplification. Neither Central America's past nor its present can be understood through simple schemes or hasty generalizations. Much less can they be appreciated using the childlike logic of the guilty and the innocent. If this work succeeds in bringing the reader to understand, to elevate his or her consciousness, to unsettle and to persuade the reader to join in the difficult task of systematically explaining the present, then it will have more than attained its goals.

San José, Costa Rica
December 1987

# Preface to the First Edition

A history of Central America. The topic itself is fraught with problems. On one hand, a shared history forces us to limit consideration to five countries: Guatemala, El Salvador, Honduras, Nicaragua, and Costa Rica. On the other hand, from a geographical viewpoint we might be expected to deal with a larger unit. The Isthmus also includes both Panama in the south and the Yucatan Peninsula in the north. The mountains of Chiapas were part of the Kingdom of Guatemala until 1821, and their continuity with the high plains of Guatemala is very apparent. Belize itself shares quite a few features, both culturally and physically, with Central America's Atlantic Coast. One could expand the geographical perspective even further to include not only the Isthmus but the Caribbean islands as well. And if we were to expand it still further, our horizon could widen to embrace what in the United States is referred to as "Middle America": Mexico, the Central American Isthmus, and the Caribbean islands, according to some; and additionally Venezuela, Colombia, and the Guianas as well, according to others.

Any of the views mentioned above can be supported by various criteria ranging from physical geography through human and political dimensions and demographics. For us to undertake a valid historical analysis of the region, however, something more than an operational definition of the region's extent and scope is required. It is essential that what we define have common social origins. The geographical frame is not in itself important except inasmuch as it conditions and reveals the lives of societies and groups. In our case, there are two possible perspectives. The first would require us to hold fast to the present political subdivisions or to those in recent history. This would define the region on the basis of a common history in the economic, social, political, and cultural senses. The second would have us regard the whole as a zone of influence or of particular strategic interests from the point of view of some national power. Changes in technology and in perceived strategic interests naturally enter into this perspective and may even give it a rather tentative character. This latter perspective emerges in varying degrees from considerations inherent in the internal development of each state, in its relations with other states, and in its responses to outside influence.

The first perspective, which we will adopt, leads us to view the region in a restrictive way limiting it to those five countries that until 1821 made up the Kingdom of Guatemala and which achieved independence under the name of the United Provinces of Central America. The other perspective commonly characterizes studies in international relations and diplomatic history and is the usual one employed in analyses of British or North American policy toward the region.

In 1985 Belize and Panama became part of the region under the perspective we will adopt. Their membership arises barely a decade ago, however. Up until the Torrijos regime (1968–1981), Panama as an independent state hardly participated in Central American politics. The same could be said of Belize until its progressive emancipation from the British Antilles allowed us to foresee even in the 1960s a participation similar to Panama's. For these reasons we have left aside any consideration of both countries' internal development, limiting ourselves rather to their major impact on Central America's destiny.

But, what is the size of the region we will be studying? The issue is a valid one as much for the Central American reader as for others. For the former there is a need to gain a sense of perspective, so difficult to achieve from inside the region. For the latter the need arises for information about a region so little known, and so frequently relegated to the shadows.

The size of the region we will study is not especially impressive: it amounts to less than 2 percent of the surface area of Latin America. These 419,000 square kilometers (162,000 sq. mi.) constitute an area smaller than Spain (505,000 sq. km., 195,000 sq. mi.) or Sweden (450,000 sq. km., 174,000 sq. mi.) and hardly more than half the total surface area of Venezuela. It is however greater than the surface area of Japan (337,000 sq. km., 130,000 sq. mi.) or Paraguay (407,000 sq. km., 157,000 sq. mi.). The region is broken up into small individual countries. El Salvador is similar in size to Israel; Costa Rica is slightly larger than Denmark; while Nicaragua—the largest of our Isthmus states—is the same size as Czechoslovakia.

Resources speak louder than surface area. The current population, somewhat greater than 21 million inhabitants, represents 6 percent of Latin America's total population. This relative population size has varied little. Toward the end of the eighteenth century, Central America had a population of almost 1 million versus the 19 million for the rest of the subcontinent. Projections indicate the region will reach a population of 64 million by the year 2025. That growth will represent an increase to about 8 percent of the total for Latin America, equivalent to Mexico's population around 1970.

The moderate economic successes one can see in Costa Rica cannot conceal the region's overall poverty. The per capita income of the region in 1958 amounted to scarcely 10 percent of that of the United States. In 1975 the situation was similar. From 1950 to the present only the per capita income of Costa Rica has managed to approach the average for Latin America as a whole. That in itself is sufficient reason to classify the Isthmus as one of the poorest and most backward parts of the entire subcontinent.

Unity and diversity constitute, in the case of Central America, a serious challenge to the historical investigator. The formation during the nineteenth century of five nation-states compels us to consider such countries as individually significant units for the purpose of analysis. The validity of this position is beyond question. There are, however, processes and points of similarity that can only be appreciated from a regional perspective. There are instances of profound overlapping among national histories within the larger Central American context. Therein arises the inescapable need to employ a comparative approach.

This sort of perspective can help us avoid two types of errors. First there is the inevitable temptation to generalize to the whole region what is most obvious, or what is most pronounced, or what is simply most colorful. Second is the need to avoid an abstract idea of a Central American nation. The history of the region ought to be the result of a comparison of processes that sets forth as much the points of convergence as the peculiarities of each individual state. These peculiarities merit as much attention as do the commonalities.

The role of international factors should be studied from the same vantage point. The region has always been regarded as having a unity in itself or as integrated into a larger entity. But the existence of policies defined in this way does not in itself guarantee a uniform result in each of the countries of the Isthmus. One peculiar situation ought to be noted, however. In such a divided, poor, and marginal region as that of Central America, the relative weight of factors arising from outside the region is and has always been much greater than their impact on much larger countries such as Brazil, Mexico, or Argentina.

What we propose is to give the reader a short history of Central America, a concise overall panorama, beginning with the sixteenth century up to the present time. This book is written for the broader public, conceived as a study that will help them to understand contemporary events in these uncertain times. The contradictions and problems of today have their roots in the past. Nor should we forget that the future—the realm of the possible or of utopias—is also tied to history. The past weighs upon Central America perhaps more so than for other regions, and it creates an aura of bitterness around each step into the future. On a recent trip I had the opportunity to fly on one portion of the journey between Mexico and Costa Rica seated beside a Guatemalan Indian woman who spoke Spanish only haltingly. As we approached Guatemala City I filled out her landing pass (the woman was illiterate). When I asked what her nationality was she seemed not to understand the question. I persevered: "Are you Guatemalan?" "No," she replied with confidence, "I'm from Totonicapán." "Do you live in Totonicapán?" I asked next. "No," she answered, "I live in Guatemala City." To get her correct birthdate and passport number, I needed to see her passport, which declared with all the pomposity and smugness typical of modern bureaucracies, that she indeed was a Guatemalan citizen. This anecdote is more than just quaint. Our conversation cannot be appreciated without understanding our history: a centuries-old past that is still alive and breathing today.

It was not easy to achieve brevity and conciseness in the writing of this book. Nor was it easy to develop an overview of the whole region without sacrificing the uniqueness of each separate nation's history. I am not at all sure I have successfully met the challenge. At any rate, I have been helped by many years of teaching and research at several universities: in El Salvador and Honduras, years ago, and in Costa Rica since 1974. Between May and August of 1984, the Woodrow Wilson International Center for Scholars in Washington, D.C., provided me the opportunity to work in both the U.S. Library of Congress and the National Archives as well as in the Center's wonderful facilities for research, not to mention its rich intellectual environment. This small work is in a way a prelude to a larger investigation of Central America during the twentieth century which began at the Center. I want finally to mention my sincere thanks to several colleagues and friends who offered comments on parts of the book or on the book as a whole: Ciro F. S. Cardoso, Carolyn Hall, Marcello Carmagnani, and Nicolás Sánchez-Albornoz. The maps were prepared by Rigoberto Villalobos and underwritten by the Vice-Rector for Research of the University of Costa Rica. As in all my works, the support and help of my wife have proven indispensable.

San José, Costa Rica
March 1985

# 1

# The Land and the People

An imposing chain of volcanoes and a variety of tropical forests standing out against the sea—these are the first facts of Central America's geography. In a land of contrasts, the most remarkable is perhaps that between the mountainous highlands of the central region, whose slopes descend in gentle steps toward the Pacific, and the sharply divided plains on the Atlantic side which cover a broad and hot climatic zone that is densely and exuberantly tropical. This counterpoint continues between fertile volcanic soils of the central and Pacific regions. The Pacific region's moderate climate evenly divided between a rainy and a dry season contrasts with the Atlantic side's treacherous paradise of lateritic soils with their unending drainage problems and the incredible abundance of microbial life. Important exceptions are some of the river valleys that make their way down from the central peaks toward the warm Caribbean waters, true oases of plantation-style agriculture.

Challenging geography? There are no navigable rivers, save one, the San Juan that forms the border between Costa Rica and Nicaragua. There are few natural deep-water seaports and travel by land has always been extremely difficult. The central highlands and the Pacific slopes make up, as the Pre-Columbian peoples well knew, the best natural environment for farming and can sustain human habitations of some density. A geography, however, that is splendidly divided up into valleys and mesas lying between vast mountain chains also imposes its own challenge to creating a sense of connectedness. The plains scarcely compensate for a fundamental disjunction between the human settlements and the geomorphology: the relative isolation of the southern part of El Salvador, the Gulf of Fonseca (south of Honduras), and the area surrounding the great lakes of Nicaragua, prevails in the end. The *Camino Real* that once linked together the Isthmus during the colonial period was, in many long stretches, barely a mule trail grandiosely called a "Royal Road." The railways, mostly built toward the end of the nineteenth century, scarcely even offered a link to the coasts for exports. Today's Interamerican Highway was constructed mostly during World War II and finally reached Panama City only in 1964. Coastal shipping was never a very effective alternative for the central high plains population centers, so far from the coasts, especially those boasting of few good ports. Flying, under the circumstances, seems the ideal choice. But it is costly and often very risky.

Earthquakes and volcanic eruptions along the Pacific side, hurricanes along the Atlantic, loom over a general landscape of misfortunes. In 1541, Santiago de Guatemala underwent its first devastation. León, in Nicaragua, was moved to a new site in 1610 to escape future eruptions and earthquakes. In 1717 an earthquake destroyed the best buildings of the colony's capital city and there were many plans to move it to a new location. There were no less than ten eruptions of the Fuego volcano, which towers over the city, between 1700 and 1773. In 1773 a new tremor struck: the magnificent architecture of Santiago de Guatemala was demolished, and three years later the colonial administration decided to move the city to the Valle de la Ermita (Ermita Valley). Managua succumbed to earthquakes in 1931 and 1972. The list is endless. Living with earthquakes and volcanoes has been an inescapable part of Central American life for centuries.

Although few hurricanes typical of the Caribbean and the Gulf of Mexico ever reach the coasts of Central America, whenever they do, catastrophe threatens vast reaches of the Atlantic slopes. This happened in 1931 when a terrible hurricane destroyed the city of Belize, and the years 1955 and 1961 saw similar events. Hurricane "Fifi" in 1974 was particularly devastating to the Honduran coast.

The Isthmus connects the two American continents facing the Caribbean islands. Is the Isthmus just a huge bridge? Is

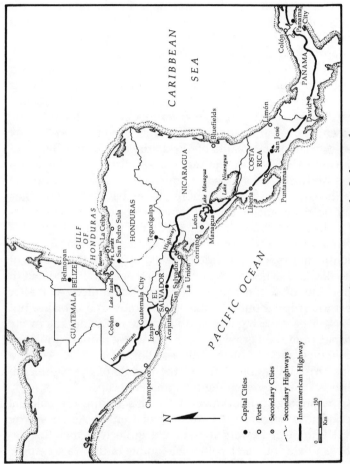

**Map 1.** The Interamerican Highway connects the Isthmus from north to south. It links the highlands all along the Pacific slopes.

it rather a continental strip that completes the vast archipelago that Columbus discovered? Or is it simply an extension of Mexico? It was historical forces more than geography which chose the last alternative. At the time of the Conquest, the cultural unity of the indigenous inhabitants extended from Central Mexico right down to the north of modern Costa Rica. The political structures of the Spanish colonization upheld this vast Meso-American unity.

Panama, located at the narrowest strip of the Isthmus and closest to South America, had its own unique destiny. It has always been a primary point of transit between the Atlantic and Pacific Oceans. Isolated from modern Colombia by the impenetrable Darien jungle, beginning in 1543 it received by sea the fabulous wealth of the Peruvian mines. Overland transport required an enormous assemblage of mules and a vast network of forts that culminated in Portobelo on the Caribbean (up to 1596 the more vulnerable Nombre de Dios had been the major port). From Portobelo each year fleets of galleons departed destined for Spain. As late as 1739, this system retained an atmosphere of chimerical fantasy: eleven months of tropical lassitude followed by about thirty days of spectacular hustle and bustle in which everything seemed to burst out of nothingness. This cycle continued year after year interrupted only by attacks of pirates and corsairs. But a slower pace arising after 1650 because of the decline in the output from the Peruvian mines gradually reduced the need for mules and supplies. The isolation of Central America thus arose bit by bit until, by the middle of the eighteenth century, the region entered a complete eclipse.

The strategic importance of Panama during the colonial period in a sense sealed the fate of Central America. The rival European powers understood quite well that the Caribbean held the most vulnerable points of that vast empire. By the middle of the eighteenth century the English had taken possession of Jamaica and were constantly prowling the Bay of Honduras. Precious woods were the motivation for establishing settlements in Belize and in Mosquitia, both of which were also centers of smuggling and harassment for the Spanish authorities. The settlement of the Atlantic Coast now added yet another contrast to the face of Central America. Since there were few Indians in the hot and inhospitable jungles, the widely separated settlements nourished their need for labor by importing African-Americans, most of whom came from Jamaica. The highpoint of the development of banana plantations and railways, reached toward the end of the nineteenth century, reinforced those patterns thanks to a renewed importation of workers from Jamaica.

The nineteenth century saw the issue of strategy replayed. First there were the conflicts between imperialist powers for the control of the interoceanic routes. There were two real options: a link through the south of Nicaragua, taking advantage of the navigable portions of the San Juan River and the great Lake Nicaragua, or the old colonial Panama route. During the second half of the century the balance of power progressively tilted toward the United States. At the close of the century the North American presence in the Caribbean had become dominant. In 1898, after the war with Spain, there was the annexation of Puerto Rico and a protectorate established over Cuba. By the Hay-Pauncefote Treaty in 1901, Great Britain freed the United States from the 1850 Compromise that had prohibited both powers from unilateral control of an interoceanic canal in the region. The Independence of Panama in 1903 and the immediate negotiation of a canal treaty completed the basic elements of a new domination. When in 1914 the Panama Canal was opened, the Caribbean had become a veritable *Mare Nostrum* of the U.S. Navy.

During the twentieth century defense of the Canal and security of such a strategic element of world trade became a permanent focus of U.S. foreign policy. From the time of Theodore Roosevelt's "Big Stick" to the Cold War years, little changed in the U.S. view of Central America. The latter was seen as a marginal area, frequently turbulent and unstable, whose "pacification" was to be assured at any cost given the strategic proximity of the Canal and the possibility of building an alternate route through another zone on the Isthmus.

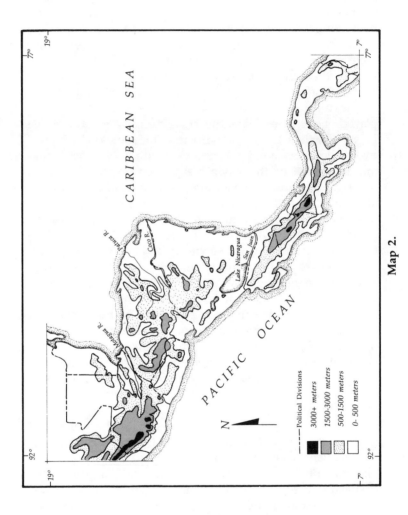

Map 2.

The Cuban Revolution of 1959 and more recently the Sandinista Revolution in Nicaragua (1979) have considerably
modified this view. The dominance of the United States now
finds itself seriously challenged, and in the last ten years the
Isthmus has experienced an era of unparalleled economic
crisis, social unrest, and strong nationalistic resurgence. All
this has elevated the problems of Central America, as varied
as they are complex, onto a level of constant international
attention.

And so one can understand the misfortune of a destiny
frequently characterized derisively by the term Banana Republics. It is a microcosm of divergent cultures and societies,
a "Balkanization" that springs from the bowels of a distant
and often unrecognized past, from the blindness of provin-
cialism and the rivalry of towns against the countryside. All
this in the face of the interests of the great powers. In the
giant chess game of shipping lanes, naval power, and military might, Central America has always been perceived geo-
politically, its significance as purely strategic.

## A PERIPHERAL AND RURAL WORLD

In strong contrast with its strategic importance are the poverty and limited economic resources that have always been
another structural fact throughout the region's history.

Farming, based on clearing land followed by successive
and periodic plowing, has been the mainstay of the majority
of the inhabitants of the region. Since the Pre-Columbian
period the cultivation of corn has been their subsistence. Su-
perimposed on this subsistence farming have been export
crops. Until the predominance of coffee in the second half
of the last century, cultivation for export exhibited a fateful
common thread of short-lived market cycles complicated by
the early exhaustion of the soil.

The plundering of natural resources is yet another enduring trait of Central American life. After the brutal extermination of the Indians came the inexorable pillage of the
forests and their wildlife. The precious woods on the north

coast of Honduras and Belize contributed in no small measure to the reconstruction of London after the Great Fire of 1666. Cutting increased in intensity during the nineteenth century, feeding a flourishing lumber industry that was run by large British and U.S. companies. Only the mountain ranges along the Atlantic Coast slowed the advancing pillage well into the nineteenth century. A rather similar devastation of natural resources took place along the Pacific Coast and particularly around the Gulf of Fonseca and the coast of Nicaragua. This selective exploitation of the forests for precious woods, rubber gum, tars, and so forth was only the initial phase of the pillaging cycle. Today sees the economic onslaught penetrate into the forests of the central mountain ranges, further constricting the extraordinarily rich wildlife of the region. Vast parts of Central America have already or will shortly become an "ecological wasteland."

The Isthmus never enjoyed a monopoly on valuable products. The costs of production and transportation of many goods compared in the long run unfavorably with similar exports by bigger producing countries. With its weak or limited integration into colonial trade, the region very early on acquired the character of a marginal province, lost even more in the hinterlands of time than of geography.

These brief and frustrated export cycles repeatedly reinforced the region's isolation and fragmentation, thereby underscoring the secular weakness of state authority, which itself has become another enduring characteristic of the region's history. The relations of social hierarchy and domination thus took on an undisguised violence benefiting the landed class almost exclusively. This overweening role of privilege can be explained in great part by the weakness of the export economy. The ruling classes had no alternative but to enter into a "zero-sum" power struggle: a savage chess match in which the gains of a few imply total loss for the many. The landholders of the colonial past, the indigo dealers of the eighteenth century, or the coffee growers of today all share this disproportionate concentration of personal privilege to some degree.

In its depth, the history of the Isthmus blends into the lives of backward, poor, downtrodden peasants inured from the beginning to eking out an existence scratching land from the mountainside. With few animals, scarcely any tools, inhabiting broken strips of land often impassable to vehicles, this sort of life was never easy and almost entirely depended on sheer effort and the generosity of the soil. Difficult travel intensified this hazardous life and buried these people for a long period in isolation and obscurity.

Race and ethnicity added a multicolor tint to the harshly exploitative relations. This racial variety is undeniable. Since the seventeenth century the African settlements on the Atlantic Coast had blended into the Pre-Columbian cultures. All were oppressed and alienated cultures whose roots to the past had been cut. The impossibility of achieving a complete cultural identity reveals one of the most subtle aspects of domination.

Beyond its exoticism, this broad range of cultures has allowed class domination to draw upon prejudice as a facade that hides and justifies the position of inferiority of the great majority of the region's inhabitants. Thus, racial prejudice never ceased to be a fundamental mechanism in the forging of the *Patria Criolla* (Creole Nation). First it guaranteed the "purity" of Spanish ancestry by contrast to Indian or *mestizo* ancestry. Later on, after Independence, it enshrined the *criollo*, that intimate blend of Spanish and *mestizo*, as the typical citizen. The exclusion of Indians[1] and blacks was an inviolable social norm (Chinese were added to the list of outcasts at the end of the nineteenth century). This exclusion found its echo well into the twentieth century in many segregation practices, both tacit and open, and in outright prohibitions.

The immense ideological power of the Catholic Church was a dominant feature of the shaping of Central American societies. As a basic constituent in colonial domination it was an effective complement to the weakness of the state vis-à-vis the enormity of personal privilege. The growth of secular power was slow and frequently fraught with difficulties. Un-

**Map 3.** Little remains of the once exuberant tropical forests; none now remain in the heartlands and the Pacific slopes. The main forests are now only in Petén and Mosquitia. Basic information was taken from H. Nuhn, P. Krieg, and W. Schlick, *Zentralamerika. Karten zur Bevolkerungs und Wirtschaftsstruktur* (Hamburg, 1975).

der the Spanish Bourbons, during the latter half of the eighteenth-century Enlightenment, there was an initial effort to strengthen state power. But it was not until the close of the nineteenth century, during the period of Liberalism and Positivism, that the triumph of secular power came to a significant degree. This triumph occurred in the state control of education and the definitive assertion of freedom of religion. Still, we should not overstate these successes. The vast majority of Central Americans continued to be illiterate, poor, and backward. And, in addition, the retreat of the Church ended the old paternalism. The anonymity that characterized contractual relationships generally replaced the old personal ties and that modicum of protection inherent in the rigid and labyrinthine social structure.

Towns, rather than cities, and an overwhelming ruralness exacerbated the relative isolation among regions and provinces, the well-known difficulties in transportation, and the dismal state of the export economy. All had developed over centuries and had scarcely begun to change in the closing quarter of the last century. Urbanization and industrialization are recent events in Central America, even more so than in the rest of Latin America as far as their impact on society as a whole.

The frontier is yet another permanent element in the life of the Isthmus. The struggle against the jungle, inexorable rains, and rugged mountains all imposed themselves on a small dispersed population. Even though there was the mirage of fabulous wealth in treasure and mines, reality imposed its own harsh, centuries-old law: the frontier was never a Promised Land. As a result, the growth of a national economy was very gradual across several centuries.

Artistic creation mirrored this intricate and backward rural world, these frozen and polarized societies. Alienation and estrangement, typical of the rural world, was found as well in the work of the major artists.

The poem *Rusticatio Mexicana*, composed in Latin by the Guatemalan Jesuit Rafael Landívar (1731–1793), resounds with images of the region's customs, nature, and wildlife.

He composed it during the financially and morally difficult times of his years in exile in Italy. Published in Módena in 1781, the poem's fifteen cantos in majestic hexameters were only resurrected at the end of the nineteenth century by Menéndez y Pelayo. They were completely translated into Spanish only in 1925. A hundred years after Landívar, Rubén Darío (1867–1916), born in Nicaragua but a citizen of the world, revolutionized the literature of Spanish America. His poetry, however, is incomprehensible without a knowledge of life in Paris, Madrid, and Buenos Aires. The more universal, profound, and remarkable the work of the poet, the more he is a stranger in his own land. This, perhaps, is one of the keys to the tragedy of Darío's life.

Scholarship offers other no less notable examples. The Salvadorean Francisco Gavidia (1863–1955) was a well-known humanist who lived in a timeless world, sitting, as if in a novel, in an imaginary eighteenth-century library or conversing with disciples and friends in Hellenic Athens. Perhaps a more talented realist writer was the Honduran Rafael Heliodoro Valle (1891–1959). Immersed in many and varied activities, he found in Mexico a favorable environment for his prodigious literary gifts. Less pretentious but more effective were the efforts of the Costa Rican teacher and journalist Joaquín García Monge (1881–1958). His journal *Repertorio Americano*, which he published from 1919 until his death, was more than a remarkable example of persistence and drive. It also constituted an invaluable contribution to critical dialogue that sought to open paths to a common identity across diverse intellectual endeavors both within the Isthmus and beyond it.

Miguel Angel Asturias (1899–1974) elevated a preoccupation with Central America to an unparalleled universality. His vast fictional panorama weaves together the lives, passions, suffering, nature, and language of the Isthmus in a completely new and original style. The leader of the movement known as "Magical Realism," he opened up, like Rubén Darío, a new modality for all of Latin America. He was, however, no stranger to exile and estrangement. He

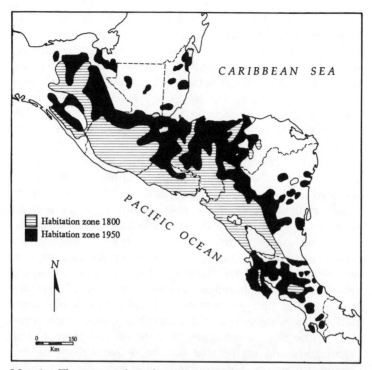

**Map 4.** There was relatively slow penetration from the Pacific side and the central highlands toward the Atlantic Coast. El Salvador by the close of the colonial period was more or less colonized. The greatest population expansion occurred in Honduras and Costa Rica. The areas populated by around 1800 are based on a list of settlements that appears in Adriaan C. van Oss, "La población de América Central hacia 1800," *Anales de la Sociedad de Geografía e Historia de Guatemala*, vol. 55 (1981). The population distribution around 1950 is based on population density maps derived from censuses taken that year.

became acquainted with the legends and religion of the Maya through a French scholar and in 1927 published the *Popul Vuh* in Paris, having translated it from a French version. Even though he spent the better part of his life outside Guatemala, he was the first to treat Central American themes in a universal style. He has unquestionably been more widely read and appreciated abroad than by those in his Guatemalan homeland who inspired his richly expressive language.

Closer to a collective endeavor, architecture and religious art reveal an authentic and less alien expression. What has survived earthquakes, eruptions, and plunder shows a profound originality, a symbiosis of the Spanish and indigenous heritages seen equally in the use of colors and materials in varied expressive forms. To a certain extent, religious art became a vehicle for the expression of popular culture. It is easy to point out the reasons for this. Religious art was a vehicle to depict daily religious practices that were both commonplace and ambiguous in their Christianity. Colonial domination was buttressed by the triumph of Catholicism; however, in the rites, ceremonies, and devotional practices the pagan gods and myths that had been overthrown by the Conquest lived on. This double level of meaning within the images and rites, their deep ambiguity, was central to the way ideological domination by colonial society took place.

Deeply sunk into a collective memory, the folkways have scarcely survived. In many instances they have completely vanished. Very few people have been interested enough to preserve in written form the diversity of dances, plays, ballads, and other popular traditions. Only a handful of ecclesiastics during the colonial period—and later some professional or amateur ethnologists, mostly foreigners—have endeavored to record them. Of what has come down to us, let us mention the *Varón de Rabinal* also called the *Rabinal-Achi*, a Pre-Columbian ballet drama from Guatemala transcribed in 1856 and published in French in 1862. The *Güegüense* or *Macho-Ratón*, a balletic farce, is recorded in the Nicaraguan dialect of Nahuatl. The latter is different from the

*Rabinal-Achi* in being purely a product of colonial society in its theme, language, and its mestizo characters. The overwhelming European influence, carried on the wave of liberalism that occurred during the latter half of the nineteenth century suffocated almost everything else. Facing the contempt of the ruling classes and the disdain of the middle classes, popular culture rooted in the colonial past survived in religious festivals and practices. Exotic archeological relics, however, attracted the ruling groups who were always ready to sell items in Europe or the United States. And so, while the great museums of the world filled new rooms with Mayan stele or beautiful jade pieces, the Central American "nouveau riche" filled their houses with chandeliers, mirrors, and marble, not to mention Greek columns, Gothic archways, and even Arabian minarets in a strange blend of styles and tastes. Live swans, European princesses, and trumpet fanfares adorned the parties and drawing-room gatherings on the eve of the World War I. With less opulence but similar drive, the middle classes emulated tirelessly those customs showing proper upbringing and *savoir vivre*. Writers of novels of manners (*costumbristas*) assured entertainment (as did magazine novels) and reassured readers that inside their idyllic world of bountiful landscapes and crystalline streams the misery of the peasants became just an unavoidable misfortune buried under richly hued countrysides and tender emotions.

With the advent of the twentieth century, mass culture penetrated deeply and decisively into the heart of Central American society. Its impact on ideology can only be compared to the change wrought by the Spanish Conquest in the sixteenth century. The strengths and weaknesses of the United States penetrated in advance of its industries, preceding the factory work ethic and the style of capitalist business organization. The middle classes radically changed their consumer patterns, adapting them fervently to the "American way of life," while the upper classes exchanged Paris for Miami. These new customs were not limited to the top of the social pyramid but permeated in varying degrees all the way to the bottom. Radio, movies, and television allied with urbanization explain why change was so swift and pervasive. Similarly these changes are reflected in the movement of workers to the United States, most of whom were illegal. Soccer replaced religious processions for the common folk in popularity. Protestant sects inveighed with equal fervor against the established Catholicism.

Urban development also brought with it, after 1950, a flourishing of middle-class culture. Theatre, literature, plastic arts, and music reached new levels and expressiveness. Even though minor compared to the cultural ferment of the great Latin American capitals, such as Mexico City or Buenos Aires, the phenomenon is significant within the context of the poverty and relative backwardness of Central America. The great variety of styles and artistic groups and the wealth of experimentation nonetheless conceals somewhat these artists' constant troubled search for their own values. Artistic creativity reveals once again, as in a mirror, a trait of larger social importance: it expresses at its heart a deep crisis of national identity.

## REGIONAL UNITY AND DIVERSITY

We shall begin with cultural geography. In reality, there are several Central Americas. In the *altiplanos*, the highlands and high plains of Guatemala, the colonial world and that of the Pre-Conquest Maya survive with all their linguistic and ethnic diversity, yet brought together in a common material culture, similar community structures, and a broad religious syncretism. In 1984 the indigenous population of Guatemala still made up almost half the total population of the country. In the rest of Central America (excluding the hills of Chiapas in southern Mexico), very little remains of indigenous Central America: just a few miserable settlements that are the objects of contempt and discrimination, and clearly in the process of disintegration.

As soon as we descend from the Guatemalan *altiplano* toward the Pacific Coast or enter into the highlands of Honduras and El Salvador, the change is dramatic. We find our-selves in a mestizo and criollo Central America. From the south of Guatemala to the North of Costa Rica along the Pacific coastal region the traits are unmistakable. Corn farm-ers (hombres de maiz), peasants, and farm laborers combine regional and Spanish features with ancestral Mayan or Mex-ican traits. From farming styles up to dress styles, daily life is infused with a common culture. Nothing is left of the in-digenous community and the umbilical link with the earth has been palpably transformed. Here and there one can find a maize field of uncertain ownership, or perhaps a small shanty in the outskirts of a town or near a large hacienda. The impersonal character of contractual relations is domi-nant and is progressively controlling every other sort of so-cial tie.

As we travel along the byways of this part of the Isthmus we encounter a constant human landscape: barefoot peas-ants with straw hats and machetes slung from their waists, walking ceaselessly along the shoulders of the main roads, women carrying bundles or jugs on their heads, and naked children with swollen bellies and restless gaze. During the harvest, trucks laden with coffee, sugar cane, or cotton min-gle with truckloads of cutters in a constant traffic. What a sight are the cities, under a blue sky and hot sun, their mar-kets bustling. The peasant is the source of everything; but how distant is this reality from the picturesqueness and colorful unhurried ritual of the plazas of the Guatemalan highlands! Nor can we neglect the visible presence of sol-diers, almost always in pairs, with their olive-drab uniforms and ever-present submachine guns. Under that misaligned helmet lurks the same mestizo face of the peasant indelibly ingrained in the memory of anyone who has wandered through this rugged land of steep mountains and valleys.

The criollo culture scarcely remains in the urban middle and rural landed classes. Very little remains in fact of the Spanish heritage so finely delineated by Stephens or Squier in the middle of the last century. A selective immigration of businessmen, mainly of Anglo-Saxon descent, invigorated the coffee industry and drastically altered the habits of the ruling class. Succeeding this new wave of Europeanization toward the end of the nineteenth century was the cultural imprinting from the United States, whose vast impact we have referred to earlier.

Traveling further south along the Pacific slopes into the highlands of Costa Rica, the essential mestizo physiognomy of Central America undergoes some change. The population is now more homogeneous and the European racial influence is easier to recognize. The cultural traits of Mesoamerica are likewise weaker: the diet of corn now shares a place with potatoes, and tortillas with bread. The climate and vegetation are also different with the rainy season longer and the countryside green all year round. Nonetheless the life of the peasant shows the same rustic simplicity, and there remains the same ceaseless movement of coffee, cotton, and sugar cane. Liquor climaxes the weekly round of work as always. True, one sees more schools, fewer soldiers, and, generally speaking, less poverty and backwardness. A telling comparison is that of harvesters in November or December: here in the south the contingents of workers harvesting coffee are not barefoot and their clothing is more varied and colorful. Bluejeans are to be found. There are more women workers than in Guatemala, El Salvador, or Nicaragua.

If we change direction and travel on the Atlantic side of Central America everything transforms again. The ebullient tropical forests and isolated worlds of the banana plantations reveal a black culture stagnating or dying, insulated from history and suffering under the power and prejudice of a criollo and mestizo Central America. From Belize south to Costa Rica we see a "black" Central America closely allied to the Afro-American Caribbean. Apart from Belize, which achieved independence in 1981, this world is one of an oppressed minority resisting integration into the cultures of the highlands and the Pacific Coast. This is a growing problem, still unresolved, facing the governments of Honduras, Nicaragua, and Costa Rica. It is further complicated by the fact that the independence of Belize, recognized by all other countries, is still not accepted by Guatemala.

This cultural diversity is a continuing burden from the past. We might say that it manifests the terrible weight of history. What, then, can we say about a "Central American Homeland"? Are these countries truly separate nations? From what does the legitimacy of their governments derive? We all know how political change outpaces changes in culture and mentality. The notion of a Central American Homeland is forming with the same rhythm that the nations formed their identities. Let us outline at least some of the basic moments of its formation.

The "Euro-American" cultural symbiosis that reigned during the colonial period represents its earliest influence. The key elements were its roots in the land and the mountains. Still, the colonial heritage is ambivalent, its language and institutions blended with separatist tendencies. The future republics were constituted upon the civil and religious administrative divisions set up toward the end of the colonial period.

The Central American Federation had a short and tragic life from 1824 to 1839. After this ill-fated beginning other similar attempts toward union shared a common trait: they were inevitably futile and provided the pretext for one republic to meddle in the internal affairs of another. During the period at the end of the nineteenth century, the coffee- and banana-exporting areas introduced new features into the regional identity, a struggle for survival and a uniformity in agrarian culture, and also the new problems of economic dependency and one-crop economies. After the end of the 1950s, industrialization added—through the Central American Common Market—further shared features. The deep economic, political, and social crises that have beset the Isthmus since the end of the 1970s are yet another vivid and shared symptom.

The Central American Homeland has been redefined several times through history and doubtless will be reinter-

**Map 5.** Native Maya-Quiché are predominant in Guatemala. In the remainder of Central America there are few of the original Pre-Columbian inhabitants, only the Lencas in Honduras, the Matagalpas in Nicaragua, and the Talamancas in Costa Rica. Linguistically, the Misquitos, Sumus, and Ramas all belong along with the Talamancas to the South American Macrochibcha family; racially and culturally they have incorporated many Afro-American elements. Negroes and mulattoes predominate in Belize and along the Honduran and Costa Rican Atlantic Coast. Basic information is based on West and Augelli, *Middle America* (Englewood Cliffs: Prentice Hall, 1976), p. 383, and Nuhn et al. atlas referred to in map 3.

preted again in the future. For the moment, "Native American" Central America and "black" Central America do not have a place in its definition.

In the modern world, the nation-state epitomizes national culture and nation-states are still considered the highest form of social evolution. Legitimacy is the key attribute of a state in its exercise of power. Legitimacy or the lack thereof is very useful as a clue to the sort of social structure that prevails and to the character of the government in power: how is authority exercised? How do individuals obey constituted authority? How legitimate is the state in the eyes of its "citizens"?

The Central American nations have their roots in the colonial period. We have already observed how their political boundaries emerged from administrative jurisdictions in the latter half of the eighteenth century. That period also bequeathed their institutional heritage. Other basic sources stem from the nineteenth century—the wars of Independence, civil strife, the restoration of conservative rule and, finally, the Liberal triumph of the 1870s. The United States, Republican France, and the Spanish constitutional experiments provided the basic models that were blended into various constitutions during this century. Once again, however, political change outpaced social change and the transformation of social consciousness.

Liberalism meant invariably that the peasants submitted to the new order governed by a worldwide coffee market. The price that was paid, expropriation, coercion, and violence, was not only an egregious "initial sacrifice." The social costs occasioned by successful development as an agricultural exporting nation were borne eventually by the whole of society. Violence and the repressive state became progressively identified with the established order. These twin elements have become, a century later, even more necessary to guaranteeing "social peace." Nothing could have been more contradictory than the ardent liberalism of the upper classes at the close of the last century. At least then there was the hope that free enterprise within a favorable legal framework would assure a different future, a gradual burial of the flagrant contradiction between the rights and duties of the citizenry, enshrined in the legal codes, and the peasantry trapped by poverty, violence, and exploitation. A half-century later those grandiose dreams went the way of Icarus. The hot sun of reality had dissolved the false premises of progress and automatic evolution. Just as for Icarus, the dream ended with a spectacular and horrible conclusion. Insurrections, death, and poverty reveal a fateful and cyclical pattern in the breakup of the landed class's role as ruling class. This is the end, if you like, of another grand "El Dorado." In this context Costa Rica shows itself the "happy exception," or perhaps a fortunate accident. It is not easy to explain under these conditions why Costa Rica gradually developed an "exemplary" representative democracy and a remarkable political stability. Rather, let us say that it defies a simple explanation. It is without question the product of a long historical process and many varied factors. In this there is some magnificent material for a study in comparative history.

Belize and Panama, at the two extremes of the Isthmus, do not entirely share Central America's history, as was noted in the Preface. They certainly contribute to making its history comprehensible. If our perspective were future-directed, we would have to deal with them. To put things in context, we will consider below some features of their histories that, up to a point, are parallel.

## PANAMA

At the southern tip the Isthmus narrows. The mountains are lower and the Isthmus butts into the continent of South America. The province of Darien, on the east, is similar in environment to northern Colombia, covered by a dense, impenetrable tropical forest. The Interamerican Highway stops at this jungle's doorstep. The population thins out now to a few thousand Cuna Indians and some Afro-Caribbean groups. Efforts at colonization have repeatedly failed in this wild forested part of the Isthmus. The Spaniards were forced to evacuate in 1520, 1598, 1621, and again in 1784–1792. A single Scottish effort lasted only from 1698 to 1700. The same happened to French colonists between 1744 and 1754. The nineteenth century saw similar efforts and outcomes.

Living conditions are far more hospitable toward the middle of the Panamanian Isthmus and in the west toward the Costa Rican frontier. Here the land is especially suitable for farming and cattle-raising and, additionally, this is the region where the Isthmus is narrowest and easiest to cross over. Panama's history and life—in three basic stages—has centered on this region since 1543. The first stage ended in 1739 when the English succeeded in taking Portobelo and the periodic fairs and transatlantic fleet ceased. The second stage unfolded in the mid-nineteenth century starting with the inauguration of the Inter-Oceanic Railway. The third began with building the current Canal and Panama's independence in 1903. Each of these three stages heralded major technological, economic, and political changes that merit study, even if only cursory.

A transportation-based economy formed toward the middle of the sixteenth century. Ore from Peruvian mines arrived by sea in Panama City on the Pacific Coast and was then transported by mules and slaves to the port Nombre de Dios (replaced by Portobelo after 1597) on the Atlantic Coast. Here it was loaded onto fleets of galleons and made its way to Spain. This system required a significant defensive network of forts and a continual supply of mules, slaves, and food all brought in from neighboring regions. These economic links lacked continuity, however, due to growing threats of pirates and corsairs, to the decline in the productivity of Peruvian mines, and to a not always very consistent colonial policy. In the latter half of the seventeenth century the trans-Isthmus traffic generally declined although it did last until Portobelo was razed by the English in 1739 and until the system of fleets was abolished in 1748. After this time, the Panamanian Isthmus entered a profound decline.

Toward the close of the eighteenth century, the population scarcely exceeded 85,000.

The cost of these shipments has been calculated by Alfredo Castillero Calvo and clearly illustrate the character of the Panamanian traffic. Per kilometer, they were the most costly of the entire colonial empire. One hundred pounds of cargo from Panama City to Portobelo cost thirteen times more than the Huancavelica-to-Potosí route and forty-seven times more than the Acapulco–Veracruz route. Therefore the choice of Panama could only be justified for cargos of precious metals. Let us note the reasons for the extraordinarily high cost. The route was difficult, but more important were the material costs of mules and slaves, which had to be imported, and the cost of defense.

The outlook for inter-oceanic transportation changed during the nineteenth century with the railway and the possibility of constructing a canal. Still, there needed to be an economic motive to make these profitable choices. First there was the California Gold Rush. In 1850 a U.S. company assumed responsibility for building a trans-Isthmus railway, which it finished five years later. Passenger and cargo transportation were very busy enterprises until 1869 when the Transcontinental Railway was opened in the United States. Panama then entered decline once again since, comparatively, transportation costs were too high. The rise of worldwide maritime trade and the successful example of the Suez Canal initiated the Panama Canal odyssey. Ferdinand-Marie de Lesseps failed (1880–1891) both financially and in construction strategy, and the Canal company ended up selling its shares to U.S. interests. In 1903 everything changed. Panama achieved independence from Colombia and the United States undertook to build the canal. The Canal Treaty involved extraterritoriality, however, and the right of intervention. When construction was concluded in 1914, the young republic was cut in half by the Canal Zone and had been transformed into a veritable U.S. colonial enclave. The whole history of an independent Panama centers on this circumstance.

Panama became independent from Spain late, on November 28, 1821. The business elite opted for union with Colombia even though not all agreed. Bolívar's Congress in 1826 barely had symbolic significance. Panama's political history during the nineteenth century is a continuing counterpoint between separatism, efforts to rebuild the old transportation-based economy, and the isolation of a poor underpopulated region.

Separatism is a recurrent feature. In 1830, 1840, and 1850 there were separatist efforts; there were also periodic calls for an English or U.S. protectorate. The Peace, Friendship, Navigation and Trade Treaty between Colombia and the United States in 1846 established the Panamanian Isthmus's neutrality and guaranteed freedom of transit. In 1855, Panama became a Federal State of Colombia and this was ratified again by the 1863 Colombian Constitution. Panama, however, could not avoid being involved in Colombia's internal conflicts. In 1885 a civil war shook the whole country and the United States intervened to assure order. When the Colombian Constitution was modified, Panama lost all its autonomy. A similar chain of events took place in 1900 during the "War of a Thousand Days." The United States once again intervened. Panama's independence and the Canal Treaty negotiations were completely parallel events during 1903. Indeed, both took place under the protection of the U.S. Navy.

Relations with the United States dominated Panamanian politics in the twentieth century. The Canal-based economy brought modernization and progress, but it also entailed a divided country that was forced in a myriad of ways to accept colonial subjection. Only a weak sense of national identity was established during the struggle to revise the Treaty of 1903. As before, the transportation-based economy reinforced its isolation. Panama scarcely maintained any economic ties with its neighbors.

In 1936, the United States unilaterally waived its right to intervene in Panama's internal affairs. It had exercised that right in 1918 in Chiriquí and in 1925 in the capital itself. The pretext for the latter was a major renters' strike. Still, the economic and military importance of the Canal had steadily grown and always was considered vital to U.S. security. Under these conditions, any modification of the Treaty of 1903 that implied any sort of sovereignty would deeply affect major vested interests and touch a sensitive nerve.

The Panamanian nationalist movement picked up special strength in 1959 and 1964 mainly under the leadership of university students. But it was when General Omar Torrijos took power in 1968 that the struggle took on a new dimension. Panama's role in the renegotiation of the Canal Treaties, concluded in 1977, was accompanied by a strong popular mobilization and an activist diplomacy that sought and found links for solidarity with other Latin American and even Third World countries. Even though not all of Panama's hopes were completely satisfied, the Canal Zone was eliminated in 1979 and Panama's complete sovereignty over its territory was recognized. In addition, significant steps were made in the difficult task of a joint operation of the Canal by Panama and the United States.

New linkages, especially with Central American countries and throughout the Caribbean basin, and a renewed national identity seem to be the most salient aspects of this latest but most crucial stage in Panama's existence.

BELIZE

Belize proclaimed independence on September 15, 1981. Thus was born the newest Central American nation 160 years later than its neighbors. It has emerged from a long colonial past and an equally long process of decolonization.

The Spanish had never occupied in any permanent fashion the present territory that comprises Belize. Missions and military expeditions attempted with relative success to conquer the Mayan tribes that were entrenched in the mountainous forests in Belize's interior all through the seventeenth century. In the middle of that century, the British buccaneers set up bases on its swampy inhospitable coasts.

Soon they dedicated themselves to cutting and exporting campeachy wood whose crimson color was so sought by the European textile industry. For the next two centuries, the British occupation followed a similar pattern of logging rare wood, first campeachy wood and then mahogany, sold through Jamaican markets. Spain never gave up its territorial rights over this region even though the Treaties of Paris (1763) and the London Agreement (1786) gave the British logging concessions. Although it began precariously, soon the British occupation was complemented by smuggling and became permanent. During the latter half of the eighteenth century several Spanish efforts to dislodge the British failed.

Logging was done primitively and was constrained by the seasons. Campeachy trees are small and grow near the coast. One cutter helped by two or three slaves could cut and remove quite a number. Things changed with the logging of mahogany, for this required more slaves and capital. Even though this situation did not follow the classical plantation economy pattern, the slavery was equally inhuman and oppressive and fugitive slaves became a frequent occurrence. By the end of the eighteenth century a handful of concessionaries held the majority of the some 2,000 slaves in the Belize territory and the rights to cutting. Since the English Crown recognized Spanish sovereignty, no one had proper titles to the land. In practice, however, there was private ownership.

With Central America's independence in 1821, Belize took on the important role of trading intermediary between Guatemala and England. Mahogany exports flourished especially between 1835 and 1847, tending to decline as the coastal forests were exhausted. By the mid-nineteenth century the British Honduras Company, later changed to the Belize Estate and Produce Company in 1875, was made up of the most prominent families and supported by London investors. It dominated practically all of Belize's economy.

Local government enjoyed some autonomy, and descendants of the original inhabitants participated in the governance. But this changed drastically in 1862 when Belize was declared to be a British colony. This change of status arose from several circumstances including the U.S. recognition of British sovereignty under the Dallas–Clarendon Agreement of 1856, as well as the prohibition of British settlements of Mosquitia and the Bay Islands. On the other hand, the Treaty of 1859 signed by Guatemala and Great Britain removed all obstacles to this change by agreeing to the boundaries and recognizing its new status.

Slavery was abolished in 1838, but the freed slaves were still subjected to particularly harsh treatment. Such practices as debt peonage, payment in tokens or scrip, and punishment by forced labor arose. Around 1870 there were several attempts to set up a plantation system primarily to produce sugar cane. These efforts were of short duration, and within the overall economy Belize continued to depend on forest products for export. Of these, the resin of the sapodilla tree, used for chewing gum, grew in importance in the 1880s. A few contingents of Chinese and Hindus joined the mixture of Antilles and Mayan Indians (originally from Yucatan and Guatemala) to make up a veritable ethnic mozaic of this growing population that still remained small in absolute numbers: slightly over 25,000 in 1861, scarcely increasing to 100,000 a century later. Racially and culturally a new sort of local mestizo was emerging who found new opportunities with urbanization and the development of trade ties with the United States, especially following World War I. The colony's modernization proceeded slowly, however, and economic diversification that included agriculture and fishing only took hold after a severe post–World War II depression.

Helped partly by English law and partly by their own struggles, salaried workers gained greater labor rights. It is important to note that labor contracts were finally removed from a criminal law framework. In the 1940s there arose an important labor movement. Belize's long arduous road to independence took place within the framework of decolonization throughout the English Caribbean possessions during the 1950s and 1960s.

In 1954 universal suffrage and a Legislative Assembly

were established. Although the Governor General retained major powers, this was a significant step toward democracy and autonomy. Ten years later, a parliamentary system was set up in which the Governor General only retained symbolic authority. Still, independence waited twenty years to arrive because of Guatemalan objections. Guatemala had claimed Belize as part of its territory on several occasions, even threatening invasion in 1963 and 1972.

Complete independence of Belize depended, in the final analysis, on international recognition. This situation changed quickly beginning in 1975 when General Torrijos, in the context of Panama's struggle for sovereignty over the Canal, allied himself with George Price, Belize's prime minister, and presented Belize's case before several international forums. Latin American solidarity with Guatemala quickly broke and the situation changed even further with the fall of the Somoza family in Nicaragua in 1979, since it had been a staunch ally of the Guatemalan military. In 1980, the U.N. General Assembly voted to recommend Belize's independence by a vote of ninety-nine for and seven abstentions. The United States accepted this resolution and in 1982 signed a military assistance and cooperation agreement with Belize.

Relations between Belize and the other Central American nations have been continuous if weak over several centuries. But this has changed with decolonization and independence. The new nation shares many structural characteristics with its neighbors in the Isthmus, although it belongs to another cultural and political tradition. A small country with a poor population and very limited economic resources, it could not easily sustain development over the long run without close cooperation with its neighbors. This cooperation includes the former British Caribbean colonies who, like Belize, have also recently achieved independence. Belize has belonged to the Caribbean Economic Community, CARICOM, since 1971. The pull of its Isthmus neighbors, such as Mexico, Panama, and the Central American countries, is singularly important and doubtless will grow. We ought to mention, as well, the settling of Salvadorean and Guatemalan refugees fleeing from their respective civil wars. This is a novel and important situation with respect to its eventual demographic consequences.

## CONCLUSION

To study the history of Central America is to ponder a fragmented "space" dominated by physical and cultural diversity. We need to consider as well stubbornly enduring conditions that frequently differ from what is better understood and easily explained. The comparative method bristles with major difficulties at each step. Nevertheless, the method is worth the effort from several points of view.

Looking into the lens of Central America, it is clear beyond a shadow of a doubt that we cannot imagine the future of the Isthmus without also imagining various forms of integration.

In the light of Central American history, Central American history has a manifold importance. It is always tempting to reconstruct the history of such a large region in terms of its largest countries, ignoring the smaller ones or, worse yet, falling into the "Banana Republics" stereotype. A detailed comparative study of societies, such as in Central America, nevertheless has its advantages. In dealing with relatively simple socieites—one could even describe them as "Micro-States" or "Micro-Economies"—many processes can be studied with exceptional simplification, a fortunate circumstance not often available to us in studying larger and more complex societies. A similar clarity occurs in observing outside influences on Central America that would be much less for larger countries. All this facilitates controlled observations and approaches to quasi-experimental situations. Exaggeration of some features, the weight of an all-too-resistant recent past, the caricaturish nature and apparent absurdity of so many aspects of Central American reality, all contribute to making our investigation an urgent but fascinating task.

Table 1   Central America: Urban Population in Cities
with over 20,000 Inhabitants as a Percentage of
Total Population

|  | 1930 | 1950 | 1960 | 1970 |
|---|---|---|---|---|
| Guatemala | 10 | 11 | 16 | 16 |
| El Salvador | 10 | 13 | 18 | 20 |
| Honduras | 5 | 7 | 12 | 20 |
| Nicaragua | 18 | 15 | 13 | 31 |
| Costa Rica | 13 | 18 | 24 | 27 |
| Latin America* | 18 | 29 | 33 | 42 |

Source: *Statistical Abstract of Latin America* (Los Angeles: University
of California at Los Angeles, Center of Latin American Studies),
vol. 21 (1981), table 634; and vol. 22 (1983), table 633.
   *The percentage for all Latin America has been calculated with
a weighting based on the total population country by country.

Table 2   Central America: Land Use in 1978 (percentage)

|  | Cultivation | | Grazing | Other* |
|---|---|---|---|---|
|  | Seasonal | Continuous | Grazing | Other* |
| Guatemala | 13.3 | 3.2 | 8.1 | 75.4 |
| El Salvador | 24.5 | 7.8 | 29.0 | 38.7 |
| Honduras | 13.9 | 1.8 | 17.0 | 66.5 |
| Nicaragua | 10.3 | 1.4 | 26.0 | 62.3 |
| Costa Rica | 5.6 | 4.1 | 30.1 | 60.2 |

Source: *Statistical Abstract of Latin America*, vol. 22 (1983).
   *Includes uncultivable land, forests, mountains, lakes, etc.

Table 3   Central America: Income per Capita
(in 1970 dollars)

|  | 1950 | 1960 | 1970 | 1980 |
|---|---|---|---|---|
| Guatemala | 293 | 322 | 417 | 521 |
| El Salvador | 265 | 319 | 397 | 399 |
| Honduras | 232 | 250 | 289 | 317 |
| Nicaragua | 215 | 271 | 354 | 309 |
| Costa Rica | 347 | 474 | 656 | 858 |
| Latin America | 396 | 490 | 648 | 870 |

Source: *Statistical Abstract of Latin America*, vol 21 (1981); CEPAL,
*Anuario Estadístico de América Latina*, 1983.

Table 4   Central America: Surface Area, Total
Population, and Population Density per Square
Kilometer

|  | Area (thousands of sq. km.) | Total Population (millions) | | Population Density (per sq. km.) | |
|---|---|---|---|---|---|
|  |  | 1950 | 1980 | 1950 | 1980 |
| Guatemala | 109 | 3.0 | 7.3 | 27 | 67 |
| El Salvador | 21 | 1.9 | 4.8 | 90 | 229 |
| Honduras | 112 | 1.4 | 3.7 | 13 | 33 |
| Nicaragua | 131 | 1.1 | 2.8 | 8 | 21 |
| Costa Rica | 50 | 0.9 | 2.3 | 18 | 46 |
| TOTAL | 423 | 8.3 | 20.9 | 20 | 49 |

Source: *Statistical Abstract of Latin America*, vol. 21 (1981); CELADE,
*Boletín Demoqráfico* 32, (1983).

# 2

# The Colonial Past (1520–1821)

## THE CENTURY OF CONQUEST

At the onset of the Spanish invasion, the Pre-Columbian civilizations showed a remarkable diversity. In the Guatemalan and Salvadorean highlands, the lowlands of Yucatan, and the Gulf of Honduras, highly populated Indian settlements existed sharing a Mesoamerican culture under the hegemony of the Mayas but with a growing influence from Mexico. East of an imaginary line beginning at the mouth of the Ulúa River in the Gulf of Honduras and ending at the immense Lake Nicaragua and the Nicoya Peninsula there were, by contrast, cultures of a Caribbean and South American type that archeologists and anthropologists refer to as the "intermediate zone" or "circum-Caribbean." Here we are dealing with less-populated settlements that are relatively separated from each other. These groups engaged in slash agriculture, cultivating tubers (especially yucca or manioc), and in various sorts of hunting, fishing, and gathering. The social organization of these groups was not only less sophisticated than that of the Mayan groups but also extremely varied including everything from bands and tribes to chiefdoms and confederations of chiefdoms.

Mexican cultures, however, had existed for several centuries and were rather dynamic at the time of the Conquest. The recent annexation of Soconusco, a commercial enclave in the Gulf of Honduras, and the presence of traders who doubled as spies in the principal Mayan cities of the Guatemalan highlands are illustrations of this dynamism. The Pipil and Nicarao cultures of El Salvador and Nicaragua, respectively, had arrived in successive migrations from Central Mexico starting perhaps as early as the ninth century. A linguistic atlas of Mesoamerica, valuable as an indicator of cultural identity, reveals a complex mosaic interweaving Nahuatl and Mayan language families along with occasional language families clearly of South American origins.

Corn, grown under a system of slash cultivation interrupted by variable periods of fallowing, and a variety of chile peppers, squash (ayote), and beans had been Mesoamerican staples for many centuries (since at least 1500 B.C.E.). There was generally political fragmentation—at least when the Spaniards arrived—with frequent wars between different Mayan kingdoms in the Guatemalan highlands. Here we see hierarchically organized and very stratified societies having a significant urban character. These urban centers were more ceremonial than commercial. Their architecture was highly developed and their knowledge of astronomy was astonishing. Wars and human sacrifice and a vast religious mythology were the traits that most captured the attention of the Spanish, but they obscured by their colorful uniqueness other features that were perhaps more dramatic but no less original. The agriculture, seemingly primitive, obeyed a deep and delicate symbiosis between man and nature. This wisdom and skill in handling nature allowed well-nourished populations to prosper, perhaps reaching contemporary levels of density in what has become contemporary Guatemala and El Salvador.

Christopher Columbus explored the Caribbean coast of Central America in his fourth trip and in 1502 made contact with the advanced Pre-Columbian cultures in the Gulf of Honduras. Except for sporadic incursions, however, the Conquest itself did not begin until around 1520. There were two converging expeditionary waves. One was from Mexico (conquered by Hernán Cortés in 1519) and the other from Panama (Balboa had crossed the Isthmus and discovered the Pacific Ocean in 1513). These were preceded by deadly epidemics of smallpox, pneumonia, and typhus that had begun to decimate the native populations.

There were no important political units on the Isthmus. The region was a mosaic of small tribal confederations, and the Spanish penetration was made more difficult by the fact that there were no large power centers to take over as had been true for the Aztecs and the Inca. There ensued twenty years of continuous struggles combined with the inevitable rivalries between groups of conquistadors for control and jurisdiction over the various territories. Royal authority and the religious missions took a long time to establish themselves, and all this prolonged the period of uncertainty and turmoil that reigned over a region and generated more hope than riches. These conditions led to the region being regarded at the outset more as a waypoint or staging area for other expeditions than as one for permanent settlement.

Pedrarías Dávila founded Panama City in 1519 and with it as a base endeavored to explore the Pacific Coast of the Isthmus. An expedition headed by Gil González Dávila explored the Costa Rican coastline in 1522 reaching as far as Nicaragua. Here it encountered Indians and gold. The latter was a compelling motive to continue the conquest. This was undertaken by Captain Hernández de Córdoba, who was sent by Pedrarías in 1524 and founded the cities of León and Granada. But as so frequently happened, the expeditionary force rebelled against Pedrarías's authority and by 1526 a civil war was inevitable. Pedrarías triumphed and dealt sternly with the rebels, applying the same measures employed against Balboa in 1517: Hernández de Córdoba was beheaded. Pedrarías remained governor of León until he died in 1531.

Once the conquest of Mexico had been consolidated, Cortés sent two expeditions toward Honduras, and soon took personal command of them. The founding of the cities of Trujillo and Puerto Caballos (now known as Puerto Cortés) in 1525 secured control of the region that Pedrarías had also been claiming from his base in Nicaragua. Meanwhile, another Cortés lieutenant, Pedro de Alvarado, penetrated into the Guatemalan highlands. He took advantage of the wars between the tribes to ally himself with the Cachikeles in order to conquer the Quiché in April of 1524. The Conquest continued its march southward subduing the Pipiles of El Salvador and penetrating into Honduras. In succession the conquerors founded Guatemala City in 1524 and San Salvador in 1525. Their control over the territories was uncertain, however. In Honduras, there was the inevitable clash with Pedrarías's forces while the resistence of the Indians was intense and growing. Deeper entry into Honduras was undertaken by Alvarado who founded San Pedro Sula and Gracias and particularly by Governor Francisco de Montejo who founded Comayagua in 1537. Still there were major uprisings among the Indians whose conquest was proving to be extremely difficult. Colonization was consolidated, nevertheless, in widely separated enclaves that were strategically situated. These enclaves allowed the colonization to proceed in later years once royal emissaries helped settle the bitter struggles for jurisdiction over the territories.

Around 1540 the Conquest had reached the central highlands and the Pacific Coast from Guatemala down to the Nicoya Peninsula (northeast of present-day Costa Rica). The fall of the Inca Empire and the fabulous wealth of Peru redirected the development of Central America. First there was an initial short cycle of devastation that reached its peak between 1536 and 1540 during which the Indians of Nicaragua and the Nicoya Peninsula were enslaved. They provided labor for trade with the Antilles passing through the Gulf of Honduras and along the Pacific Coast of Nicaragua, Panama, and Peru. Very little remained after those first years of desolation of the peoples and cities that the first conquistadors had witnessed during the decade of the 1520s. From 1543 Panama completely replaced the rest of Central America as the preferred route for traffic crossing the Isthmus, and mules replaced Indians as beasts of burden. Panning for gold had been somewhat profitable in Honduras and Nueva Segovia in the north of Nicaragua but declined as a source of wealth. It added new and powerful incentives to enslave the Indians, however, decimating even further their declining numbers. Toward 1560 all the easy riches were exhausted while civil and religious controls had greatly increased. Colonial life had acquired firmer and more enduring characteristics.

The Spanish settlement concentrated in the central highlands and on the Pacific slopes. Here the climate was more favorable, but above all the native population was more numerous and more easily subjugated. Despite some efforts at permanent settlements, the tropical forest lands of the Atlantic slopes remained an enormously difficult frontier with an intolerable climate, fierce Indians, and phantom riches. In fact, Spanish control was limited to a narrow coastal strip between the Bay of Amatique and the Port of Trujillo (in the Gulf of Honduras), around the mouth of the San Juan River in Nicaragua, and along the Atlantic Coast of Costa Rica between the Matina and Banano Rivers. The strategic importance of these settlements contrasted with their small foothold on the long expanse of blue and emerald-green Caribbean coastline. They were, in effect, ports connecting the provinces that made up the kingdom of Guatemala, important to the convoy fleets plying the Veracruz–Havana–Seville triangular route. They also allowed for coastal trade through the Gulf of Honduras or between Costa Rica, Portobela, and Cartegena. The vessel "Nao de Honduras" (Honduras' vessel) either joined or abandoned the fleets as the case might be to set in at Trujillo, Puerto Caballos, or Santo Tomás de Castilla. The traffic of people and commerce was in any case risky and often sporadic owing to the difficulties of overland transport and to the menace of pirates and corsairs in the Caribbean whose control had become ever-more disputed since the debacle of the Invincible Armada in 1588.

Political organization tended to stabilize during the second half of the sixteenth century. The *Audiencia*, a tribunal established in Santiago de Guatemala in 1548, had acquired since 1570 jurisdiction that would last over the whole colonial period and extend from Chiapas down to Costa Rica. Its president also fulfilled the functions of Captain General and Governor. Nominally subordinate to the Viceroyalty of New Spain (Nueva España) in Mexico, in reality the colonial bureaucracy dealt directly with the capital where all the officers were appointed. The "Kingdom of Guatemala" (Reyno de Guatemala) constituted therefore a relatively autonomous political unit shaped foremost by the jurisdiction of the *Audiencia*.

Administrative jurisdictions changed relatively little until the end of the eighteenth century and responded more to the pressures and vested interests exerted by local groups of colonizers than to any strategies for domination or control of the colonial bureaucracy itself. As a result, political and administrative power tended to split off into a diversity of nuclei all of which were equal in stature and reported to the Audiencia: at the close of the sixteenth century there were four *Gobernaciones* (provinces), seven *Alcaldías Mayores* (see maps 8 and 9), and eleven *Corregimientos* (various types of judicial and administrative jurisdictions).

Local interests enjoyed solid representation in the *Cabildo* (town council). Although the method of selection of their membership varied over the years, ranging from direct election by landowners to purchase of a seat (begun in 1591), these municipal councils not only administered municipal affairs, but often clashed with royal officials or petitioned for alterations of laws they considered harmful. That they had close ties with commercial interests in every locale, there is no doubt. Their closed oligarchic character, as a clique exclusively representing the original settlers and their descendants, is frequently exaggerated. Webre's study of the *Cabildo* of Guatemala City in the seventeenth century, however, shows that its membership (*regidores*) was primarily Spanish-born recent arrivals with close ties to merchants.

The marked domination by local interests favored, on the one hand, regional fragmentation and, on the other hand, a concentration of economic power and privileges (especially mercantile) in the city of Santiago de Guatemala.

The settlement of the Christianized Indians into towns (reducciones) and the enforcement of the New Laws (Leyes Nuevas) of 1542 was another essential feature of the way colonial life was being structured during the latter half of the sixteenth century. Bishop Marroquín and the Dominican Friars succeeded in settling the Christianized Indians in

Chiapas, Guatemala, and Honduras during the 1550s. López de Cerrato, who was the dynamic president of the Audiencia from 1548 until 1555, fought against the enslavement of the Indians with some success. He also settled the Indians into towns in Nicaragua and El Salvador.

These Christianized Indians were forced to fulfill two obligations: payment of tribute and the allocation of their labor. The first was ordinarily paid in kind and collected directly by the Crown. A part of this tribute was given over to the former royal agents (encomenderos) as compensation for their custody of the Indians. The second replaced, with some misgivings, their direct enfeoffment in service or labor. These Indians also had to contribute periodic contingents of laborers to work in the mines, on the haciendas (plantations), in building projects in the towns, and in loading and transporting goods. Those who received the benefits of these services were required to pay for them with a salary. Even more significant than the fact that the Indians were to be paid for their labor, more heeded in theory than in practice, was the fact that the allocation of their labor was handled by the colonial bureaucracy. The demands and pressures generated by private interests wove an endless pattern of petitions, concessions, and denials that were difficult if not impossible to monitor in the context of a decimated and declining native population.

Tribute in kind was pivotal, perhaps the central axis around which the whole economy of the Kingdom of Guatemala revolved. The Christianized Indians had to contribute yearly to the Crown payments in cocoa, corn, wheat, hens, honey, and so forth, as was provided for by the Audiencia's assessments. The former *encomenderos* enjoyed a percentage of this payment, generously allowed by the Crown; but as the years went by this special privilege arising from the early period of Conquest was difficult to bequeath to one's heirs and became less important. For example, in 1698 there were in the whole "Kingdom of Guatemala" 93,682 tribute-paying Indians of which 32,959 were fulfilling obligations in 147 encomiendas while the other 60,723 contributed payment directly to the Royal Treasury or to the Church. A century later the Indians required to pay tribute had risen to 114,234, but there were no further allocations by encomiendas.

The organization of the settlements blended pre-Conquest indigenous traits with a typically Hispanic administration creating a broad arena for cultural symbiosis. The subjection of the native peoples took on very complex forms and combinations, but one can perhaps summarize its character as follows:

1. The Indians enjoyed autonomy in their daily life and in the internal structuring of their settlements, under the watchful eyes of the missionary priests.
2. The chiefs and other leaders made up a native council (cabildo) and were responsible for each settlement's internal order and administration of justice, the collection of tribute, and organizing the allocation of labor and services.
3. By royal authority, the *Corregidor de Indias* (Regent of the Indies) or alcalde mayor collected the tribute and distributed it among its various beneficiaries and thereby regulated the operation of the system.
4. The Audiencia and certain officers, visiting justices, and others watched over the enforcement of the law and at least theoretically righted injustices and abuses against the Indians.

There were two conditions that allowed this complex social architecture to flourish and persist. The first is ideological in character, the second demographic. The Church and Christianization not only often mitigated the harshness of exploitation but created the necessary submissiveness and acceptance. The new value system was initially interwoven with the pre-Conquest rituals and cults but inculcated the belief that domination was a gift from Heaven. The second condition related to the inexorable decline in the native population, differing region by region in its extent, and suggested objective requirements for native settlements to sur-

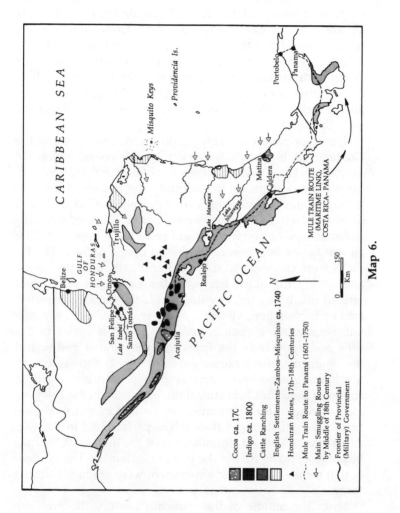

**Map 6.**

Legend:

- Cocoa ca. 17C
- Indigo ca. 1800
- Cattle Ranching
- English Settlements–Zambos-Misquitos ca. 1740
- ▲ Honduran Mines, 17th–18th Centuries
- --- Mule Train Route to Panamá (1601–1750)
- ⇩ Main Smuggling Routes by Middle of 18th Century
- ∿ Frontier of Provincial (Military) Government

Map labels:

CARIBBEAN SEA

*Providencia Is.*

Misquito Keys

Belize

*GULF OF HONDURAS*

Trujillo

San Felipe
Lake Izabal
Santo Tomás
Omoa

Acajutla

Realejo

PACIFIC OCEAN

Lake Managua

Lake Nicaragua

Matina
Caldera

Portobelo
Panamá

MULE TRAIN ROUTE
(MARITIME LINK),
COSTA RICA– PANAMA

N

0    150
Km

vive and multiply. Even though their decline in numbers responded in great measure to biological pressures—the "bacteriological unification of the world"—the toll inflicted by pressures for a labor force and the conditions of their life as laborers was likewise terribly devastating. Put in other terms, there seems to have existed for the native settlements a critical population density beneath which the settlements began to disappear or lose their distinctive character and become rather settlements of foreigners (mestizos, mulattos, and so forth) made up of all manner of castes including even poor Spaniards.

The colonization of Verapaz, on the Atlantic slope of the Guatemalan highlands, deserves special consideration. In 1537, Friar Las Casas managed to obtain royal authority allowing the Dominicans to undertake the peaceful Christianization of this region, which the Spaniards called the "land of wars." Here the Indians would not be allocated into custodial groups (encomiendas) and were to be protected from all manner of interference by the European settlers. The Indians were successfully subjected and gathered into towns, and during the initial ten years the Las Casas experiment offered much to admire within a colonial context characterized by exploitation, violence, and terror. But after 1547 matters became more complicated. Las Casas returned to Europe and apparently the friars lost their initial zeal just at the moment when pressures from the conquistadors in neighboring areas were increasing. It proved impossible to continue peaceful Christianization, especially in the Petén region, owing to the unconquerable Lacandon and Itzá resistance. The missionaries themselves participated in the war. As the years wore on, the situation of the Indians of Verapaz began resembling that of the rest of Guatemala. The vestiges of that somewhat utopian experiment were gradually effaced forever.

From the middle of the sixteenth century the pre-Conquest crop of cocoa that the Spanish had begun to savor, especially in New Spain, began to be exported profitably, particularly from the area around Izalco (in El Salvador). Its production was in the hands of the native communities and was given over as tribute to royal agents and merchants. The village of Sonsonate was a center of production: "[there] are over three hundred inhabitants and here there is much trade in clothing and cocoa,"[1] says a 1594 report. The production existed all along the coast of Guatemala reaching up into Soconusco (in Chiapas). The high point, especially in the 1570s, was nonetheless of short duration and paralleled the fate of the Honduran silver mines. The exploitation of the minerals discovered after 1569 around Tegucigalpa was difficult, and there was always an inverse relationship between the number of producing mines and the number of claims: in 1581, for example, there were over 300 claims filed yet there were only three or four producing mines. The shortage of laborers, the difficulty in storing mercury, the lack of suitable technology and of qualified staff among other considerations, explain the brevity of their profitability (from 1575 to 1584) and the stagnation in their productivity at a mediocre and declining level (annual average production of 7,000 marks up to 1610 and less than 5,000 marks afterward).[2] By comparison let us note that the productivity of the Zacatecan mines in Mexico greatly exceeded 100,000 marks annually. Shortages in labor, high costs of shipping, and the overall high and uncompetitive costs of production all provided a frustrating end to these initial efforts to export production of cocoa and silver. This state of affairs would be repeated without a break in Central America up to the latter half of the nineteenth century.

The native population was afflicted by epidemics, particularly the great one of Matlazáhuatl of 1576–1577, and by the harsh conditions of their work and daily life. Their numbers decreased steadily throughout the latter half of the sixteenth century. That population vacuum, especially severe in Nicaragua and around the Gulf of Nicoya, fostered Spanish immigration and settlements in the highlands of Costa Rica. The founding of Cartago in 1564 ends the first stage of the Conquest. From north to south, in the highlands and along the Pacific slopes, colonial domination was complete.

The same was not true, however, along the tropical forests on the Atlantic Coast. For several more centuries these would continue to have a rough frontier character and remain unexplored and dangerous.

## THE SEVENTEENTH-CENTURY DEPRESSION

At the close of the sixteenth century the colonial structuring of Central America had acquired a more defined physiognomy whose lasting traits are best described region by region.

In Guatemala, El Salvador, and some areas in western Nicaragua, the Indians continued to have a very visible presence despite their severe decline in numbers. Here as a result there could endure a "typical" colonial society replete with Spanish cities and town, haciendas or plantations, and Indian settlements from whom there was tribute and also forced labor. These features persisted through the end of the colonial period.

Over most of Honduras and in the northwest part of Nicaragua the native population had become greatly depleted and scattered. This was a region wealthy in minerals that, however, was difficult to exploit. Cattle ranches became an alternative to mineral production. It was probably the only option available to the Spanish colonizers in that vast inhospitable region with its small towns and lying almost outside the Spanish trade and political system.

Along the coastline of the Gulf of Fonseca (south of El Salvador and Honduras and north of Nicaragua), in significant areas of western Nicaragua, and in the north of Costa Rica (Guanacaste), cattle production on the large haciendas had more chance of success, being favored by the geography of the region. Overland cattle drives were relatively easy and required less labor. This region supplied beef and related products to the rest of Central America and most particularly provided the mules necessary for Panama's interoceanic traffic.

Where the herds were driven and how much cattle went back and forth depended naturally on which centers were most profitable. Up to the second half of the seventeenth century, Panama's markets reigned supreme. Later, decline in the fairs at Portobelo and the threat of piracy combined to shift the centers, and this had a lasting impact. Now the movement of the herds was northward supplying Guatemala and El Salvador, whereas the Central Valley in Costa Rica was the southernmost center. From the Gulf of Fonseca to the Gulf of Nicoya, there was a cattle-producing corridor watched over by the lakes and volcanoes of western Nicaragua that was to become an integral part of Central American life.

In the Costa Rican central highlands colonization took on its own peculiar character. This was an isolated area with few Indians and an equally small number of Spanish colonists who stayed and had to dedicate themselves to subsistence agriculture. The Central Valley had the features of a frontier. Beyond Cartago in the forests of the Talamanca Mountain range there were warlike Indians who remained unvanquished. All attempts to conquer them failed during the seventeenth century, and this fact underscored the singularity of this colonial province of Costa Rica. Its governor, Fernández de Salinas, could address the King in 1651 with these words:

> [I]n this Province of Costa Rica there are scarcely eight hundred Indians remaining wherewith we are extremely poor, and in the income Your Majesty receives you see the evidence; indeed with the over one thousand ducats that remain in Your Royal Treasury here, there is not sufficient to pay the salaries of the Governor and the priests.

These traits mentioned above had become visible by the end of the sixteenth century and became ever more pronounced throughout the long depression of the following century. Brief peaks in the export primarily of indigo, cocoa, and silver did not reduce the region's isolation. Central American life was becoming progressively stagnant.

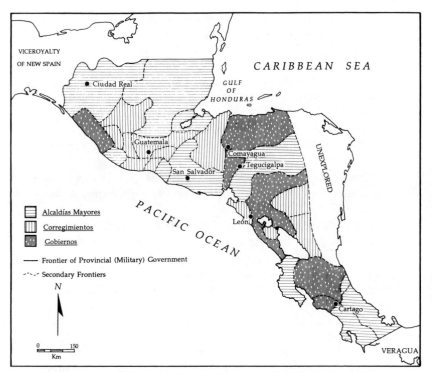

**Maps 7, 8.** These two maps depicting colonial administrative organization show how the current nations became slowly defined. They also reveal the extraordinary variety and rather great confusion of administrative and political jurisdiction.

Up to about 1650, Central America was a mosaic of administrative units, governing bodies and magistrates (*Alcaldias Mayores, Gobiernos, Corregimientos*). At the close of the eighteenth century, the situation is simpler thanks to the effects of the regulations governing Quartermasters General (*Ordenanza de Intendentes*) of 1785–86.

The Kingdom of Guatemala's economy kept going thanks to the basic spokes of colonial domination. Its base centered on subsistence production. In the Indian settlements, the haciendas and ranches, the cities and towns that were isolated and stagnant, self-sufficiency ruled everyday life. Next were the regional markets: cattle, hides, and tallow; cotton from the coast for the highlands; supplies for mining in those inhospitable desolate areas and so forth. Finally there was foreign trade. Little was left to export; there were problems everywhere. Above all, there was an overwhelming need for imports ranging from mercury and all types of equipment and tools for mining to the wine and oil required for conducting Mass.

The kingdom survived on tribute from the Indians. This provided in the seventeenth century over 70 percent of fiscal resources. But since the major part of the tribute was paid in kind, tribute provided the good for local trade and for consumption by the cities, in particular corn, wheat, cotton, wool, cocoa, yarn, and thread. Public auctions handling these products generated cash for the Royal Treasury and thereby funded public salaries and other expenses as well as remittances back to Spain (the latter exceeded 100,000 pesos annually between 1647 and 1666) The *corregidores* (presiding civil officers) and *alcaldes mayores* [judicial officers governing several adjacent towns] added a new mechanism for exploitation of the Indians, officially forbidden but never entirely erradicated, which was especially significant in Guatemala. The key was the "regulated distribution of products," which consisted of the distribution of cotton to make thread combined with the requirement to hand over all thread and yarn produced, and the forced sale of certain products. This system, besides generating fat profits for some, had two purposes. It assured the production of certain goods, such as thread and yarn and textiles; and it forced the native trading to become money-based. Indian trade was especially vigorous in the Guatemalan highlands and even reached into the capital where it was not a rare sight to see Indians going door to door selling fish from Lake Atitlán.

Uprisings and rebellions were a frequent response by Indians subjected to the pressures and tribute exacted by the alcaldes, corregidores, and the clergy. Of special note was the rebellion of the Zendal Indians in the Chiapas highlands in 1712. Thirty-two Indian settlements were involved and the rebellion was particularly violent. For over six months the Zendals repelled troops sent from Tabasco and Guatemala. The Zendals were clear about their intentions to liberate themselves from Spanish control. Repression by the Spanish was harsh enough to terrorize the rebellious communities with forced resettlements and wholesale executions.

In the overall economy of the kingdom, the allocation of native labor weighed less heavily than did payment of tribute or the regulated distribution of products. Native labor was clearly essential in the district surrounding the local capital of Santiago de los Caballeros. The indigo plantations along the coastal strip of El Salvador and the north of Nicaragua did not derive benefit from native labor until 1737, whereas for the Honduran mines its was a barely efficient method for supplying a labor force throughout the entire colonial period. In fact, in both sectors, just as in the cattle industry, the use of mestizo laborers, paid wages but kept in debt to their employers, occurred earlier than anywhere else.

Before it could coin its own money in 1733, the isolated Kingdom of Guatemala suffered from a chronic and singularly intense shortage of money. Weakness in export production paralleled the difficulties of transporting goods abroad. After 1640 the crisis in Spanish naval power in the Caribbean made the region more and more inaccessible. At the same time smuggling was beginning to occur but had yet to become well developed. Given these circumstances and the decline in the production of cocoa, a favorite product in Mexico, trade with Peru became vital. Although trade with

Peru had been forbidden at several times, it was finally allowed under several restrictions throughout the seventeenth century. This commerce brought in wine and minted coinage in exchange for the indigo demanded by the Peruvian weavers.

The Church was an essential part of colonial society. Not only did it represent the spiritual dimension of the Conquest as well as an instrument for ideologically controlling the colonized Indians, but its economic power, with its resources and properties, was immense. The secular clergy was beholden to royal authority and was organized into four bishoprics: Chiapas, Guatemala, Honduras, and León. The religious orders (Dominicans, Franciscans, Bethlemites, and the most powerful, the Order of Mercy) were charged with Christianizing and maintaining missions on the frontiers, not to mention their administration of numerous schools, hospitals, and houses of charity. The state handed over to the Church a portion of the tribute while the entire non-Indian population was forced to pay tithes. Donations by individuals of land or income in perpetuity were especially important. Nevertheless a portion of these resources were returned to the productive sector since the Church was the period's principal financial agency.

Confraternities and brotherhoods fulfilled an important role in preserving religiosity and involving the faithful in religious observances. Here we are dealing with associations approved by the local bishop and dedicated to venerating a patron saint. These associations cut across class and were represented in every parish, but they acquired particular significance in the Indian settlements. Donations and alms provided nontaxable material support; these included cash, haciendas, and cattle. The flow of wealth into these associations (the cash earned interest) underwrote the expenses of religious activities, building and maintenance of churches and sanctuaries, organizing festivals, and celebrations. On his trip through Guatemala, Thomas Gage (1625-1637) asserted that:

Also, every company or sodality of the saints or of the Virgin has two or three *mayordomos* who collect from the town alms for the maintaining of the sodality. They also gather eggs about the town for the priest every week, and give him an account of their gatherings, and allow him every month, or fortnight, two crowns for a Mass to be sung to the saint.[3]

This meddling by the clergy was on the rise and was repeatedly attacked throughout the eighteenth century as part of the many abuses perpetrated against the Indians.

The confraternities' social and economic importance grew to the point of becoming the pivotal axis of religious and cultural life. Their economic impact was no less significant. For example, in 1774 the diocese of Guatemala (which also included El Salvador) had 122 curates and almost 2,000 confraternities and brotherhoods, which possessed a patrimony valued at close to 300,000 pesos with over 50,000 head of cattle.

In the religious life of these institutions there was ample scope for a cultural symbiosis combining Christian with Indian forms of religiosity. Fuentes y Guzmán underscored this in his *Recordación Florida* at the close of the seventeenth century, but not without some apprehension:

> . . . and so also today they celebrate festivals in honor of the saints that they call *Guachibales*; dancing around with an intensity we will talk about later, dressed out in the same garb they used in their pagan past: but their songs, limited to praise of the saints recounting and reenacting their miraculous deeds, are composed by their priests. However, in their heathen sacrifices, after having perfected them in their savage ceremonies, they separate into their families and return to their dwellings jubilant and happy to end the fasting that has anticipated the moment; since they had prepared abundant and diverse victuals, which at the Crown's expense had been given over as public charity, and into which they then threw themselves with excessive and bestial gluttony, especially the great quantities of chicha.

The Spanish retreat in the Caribbean had deep repercussions in Central American life. First came the pirates and

corsairs that since the end of the sixteenth century had become a constant threat to the fleets laden with the treasures
of Mexico and Peru, anxious for booty along a coast almost
unprotected beyond its natural barriers. Next came new permanent colonizations seeking an enduring lucrative trade.
The English began their colonization in 1624 with Saint Kitts
and ended in 1655 with the taking of Jamaica. The Dutch
entered the Lesser Antilles during the 1630s but were soon
sidetracked by the possibilities awaiting them in northeast
Brazil (Recife was occupied from 1630 to 1654). France colonized the islands of Martinique and Guadeloupe in 1635.

The entry of other European powers into the Caribbean
not only broke the back of Spanish hegemony but also initiated two fundamental changes: (1) the movement from piracy and pillage to smuggling; and (2) the renewed interest
in exporting and the cultivation of certain tropical products
which brought a new sort of colonial exploitation already
begun in Brazil. This was the slave plantation. At the close
of the seventeenth century the face of the Caribbean could
not have been less like the one it displayed only a century
earlier. Those majestic Spanish galleons no longer ruled the
sun-drenched Caribbean sea. The black slave trade was in
full swing with the African population of the islands exceeding 100,000 slaves. At the end of the eighteenth century
this population had easily surpassed 1 million. The plantations had become seized with a commercial fever. Sugar was
conquering Europe. The backbreaking labor of the plantation extracted that new white gold from the dark dispair of
the African slaves. The Atlantic Coast of Central America was
slowly changing into a pallid reflection of the New Antilles.

Pirates appeared from time to time on both the Atlantic
and Pacific Oceans. Especially lethal were the attacks by
Davis in 1665 and Gallardillo in 1670 on Granada and the
sack by Olonés of San Pedro Sula in 1660. The tropical forests of the Atlantic Coast, however, provided a good natural
defense for the central highlands. English settlements were
a far greater challenge to Spanish control. The colonization

of the island of Providencia (Providence Island) off the coast of Nicaragua in 1631 was the first. The next was the English occupation in 1633 of Cape Gracias a Dios and their entry into the Miskito coastline. Even though efforts to create a plantation economy failed and the Spanish were swift in their response to these incursions (in 1641 the English were thrown out of Providencia), their presence endured for more than two centuries. Logging of precious woods, piracy and pillage, and finally smuggling and contraband were lucrative activities that proved difficult, almost impossible, for the Spanish authorities to control. The English had excellent allies in the native Miskito Indians. They intermarried quickly with the African slaves brought in for the first settlements, even including the survivors of a Portuguese slaver shipwrecked off the coast in 1641. They were therefore called *zambo-mesquitos* (or *mosquitos*, a corruption of their indigenous name already observable in the eighteenth century), and they soon shared the same hostility toward the Spanish. The English took revenge for having been expelled from Providencia by razing Trujillo in 1643. But the key event was no doubt their taking of Jamaica in 1655. From their island base, the network of English colonial settlements along the Central American coastline could count on all they needed: protection, resupply, and a good middle market for their export products.

In the 1660s the logging of precious woods extended into the Yucatán coast along the Bay of Honduras. From these logging activities the settlement of Belize would arise in the eighteenth century.

By the end of the seventeenth century the Kingdom of Guatemala was barely more than a forgotten outpost of a declining empire. As if that were not enough, added to this environment of mediocrity and poverty were the afflictions of plagues, epidemics, and hunger and shortage of food between 1680 and 1690, not to mention the earthquakes of 1688. Pirate attacks and the incursions of the *zambo-misquito* Indians increased at the end of the century and the beginning of the next. The major earthquakes of 1717 climaxed these misfortunes. The kingdom's capital city itself suffered the loss of its greatest buildings.

## THE ENLIGHTENMENT

Economic recovery combined with social and political change were the keynote of the eighteenth century. Still, it was not until 1730 or even 1750 before one could clearly perceive the reality of the changes. The recovery came slowly. It came partly from an overall favorable economic climate, especially throughout all of colonial America, and partly from the political policies of the new Bourbon dynasty in Spain. The signs are unambiguous. The population was growing continually. Immigrants were arriving from Spain and other parts of the Americas. The mestizos and criollos increased in numbers proportionately faster than any other social and racial category, but the numbers of tributary Indians of the Guatemalan highlands also increased. Production and trade rebounded notably; smuggling and contraband provided a viable alternative for a region that had been excluded from the main currents of trade with Spain. The renewal could be seen also in the colonial administration and in social change. The Enlightenment slowly penetrated the educational system and city life. Still the wave of transformation was not uniform and was frequently beset with inconsistencies and interruptions. The War of Jenkins' Ear from 1739 to 1748 between Spain and England slowed the growth of trade while the expulsion of the Jesuits seriously hampered cultural development. Political vicissitudes did not prevent prohibitions and persecutions of the "enlightened." For instance, the Sociedad Económica de Amigos del País (Society of the Friends of the Homeland) created in 1794 was suspended in 1799. Its restoration in 1810 was brought about by the new Liberal government recently installed in Spain.

The changes in the appearance of the Kingdom of Guatemala at the end of the eighteenth century were by any standard striking and strongly contrast with its prostration only a century earlier. Guatemala City had been moved after the earthquake of 1773 to its present site in the Valle de la Ermita, where it indisputably dominated the country's business and government.

From north to south, regionalism and local diversity seemed to have given way to the domination of the capital city. This had become the crossroads of monopolistic business and the heart of a state that was becoming more powerful than ever before. The English had a foothold in Belize and Mosquitia, but they were seriously restricted now in their territorial ambitions. Trade through the Bay of Honduras bore the stamp of a Spanish presence. The rise of the indigo trade sustained and highlighted the colonial prosperity that climaxed in 1790. The creaking decline and decay after this date does not lessen the peculiar character of that period. This crisis would rather exacerbate even more the differences and contradictions underlying the complex tapestry of regional life.

From the first half of the eighteenth century the Bourbons pursued four complementary policies: (1) reopening Honduran mining operations spurred by the discovery of rich new deposits in Yuscarán and Opoteca; (2) rebuilding transoceanic trade routes while not curtailing expenditures in the infrastructure of ports and roads and related projects; (3) creating a new fiscal policy that not only substantially altered the taxing structure of the economy but also led to reinvestment of surplus government revenues in defense projects and infrastructure; and (4) beginning continued efforts to dislodge the English from their Atlantic Coast settlements and thereby breaking once and for all their dominance in trade and their active smuggling network. To accomplish all this it was necessary that the state and its functionaries become preeminent as much over private business and landholding interests as over the power of the Church. Even beyond this, centralization of government grew gradually as a mental attitude in the minds of the colonial bureaucrats and became a true raison d'etre of faithful service to the Bourbons. This transformation is difficult to achieve in societies grown accustomed to being isolated and controlled locally with meagre perquisites of office.

Reinvigorated mining and a newly established mint in Guatemala (1733) favored trade with Peru and Nueva España while at the same time diminishing the dependency on minted money from El Callao. But it was not until the middle of the century that the new surge in the indigo trade provided a more stable basis for significant economic growth. On the one hand, Honduran mining operations became less important because of the usual key problems: shortage of labor, insufficient mercury, and primitive technology. In short, the prohibitive costs of production far exceeded earnings except for a few easily mined initially rich lodes and reduced the possibility of large-scale mining to barely subsistence level. On the other hand, their relative proximity to the Atlantic Coast and the difficulties of obtaining supplies by legitimate means led quite naturally to smuggling. The existence of smuggling was tirelessly recorded by the Guatemalan authorities. It could count on the permissive, and often grateful, attitude of the Comayagua official, however.

Indigo replaced cocoa as the main agricultural export after the middle of the seventeenth century. Indigo was grown on the Pacific slopes and coast from Guatemala down to the Nicoya Peninsula with most of the processing done in the present-day republic of El Salvador. Demand for this dye originated in the colonial textile mills of Peru. It was a dye that, as Sahagún once said, "gives a deep resplendent blue color." The second phase arose at the start of the eighteenth century when the English textile industry gained the forefront as a consequence of the Industrial Revolution.

Production of indigo was largely in the hands of a few major landowners who accounted for a third of the total harvest. A number of "small-scale farmers" running small- to medium-sized family operations made up the remainder. All of them were overwhelmed by a tangle of active vested interests that were often insatiable. Additional difficulties lay in the cost of shipment and the tax burden. The marketing and sale of indigo remained in the hands of a small closed monopoly of traders headquartered in Guatemala who advanced money and supplies to the growers. The result was that the revenues the growers received often did not make up the cost of production. This imbalance spurred fraud, such as the adulteration of the dye to increase its bulk, and growing confrontations between growers and traders. On top of these financial woes came devastation from locusts on several occasions (1769, 1773, 1800, and 1805). The colonial administration attempted to intervene in 1782 by setting up a Reserve Fund for Indigo Growers Society (Monte Pío de los Cosecheros del Añil) in the hands of the smaller growers, financed initially by a loan from the tobacco monopoly and used to underwrite production. But in fact the large producers were the only ones to benefit.

The indigo market collapsed at the turn of the century for reasons that are well documented. The growth in demand spurred development of production in other areas (Venezuela, India, and the Dutch Antilles), rendering Central American indigo uncompetitive on the international markets.

Despite these difficulties indigo was still the major export from Central America, until the rise of coffee, well into the nineteenth century. The golden era of the indigo markets from 1760 to 1790 laid an indelible stamp on Central American life and promoted a complex of regional links. These in turn are, in large measure, as much a source of the frustrations and bitterness of separatism as they were the forces uniting the five countries. This surge in indigo production and the retreat by the English from the Bay of Honduras also heightened the supremacy of the traders and businessmen centered in Guatemala City.

Their dominance was in no way limited to the control of overseas trade. Their commercial network extended throughout the whole regional economy: native textiles from the Guatemalan highlands, Salvadorean indigo, Honduran silver, and the cattle and mule ranching along the old established grazing corridor reaching from the Gulf of Fonseca to the Nicoya Peninsula. The "provincials" often commented on the parasitical nature of that monopoly, but its effect of tightening regional ties is undeniable. The monopoly enjoyed by this business clique was strongly reinforced beginning in 1793 by the creation of the Consulado (Administrative Office for Resolution of Commercial Disputes). The monopoly particularly hurt anyone who required imported commodities (such as mercury or tools) or who desired luxury imports such as furniture and clothing, and consumables such as wine, olives, and so forth. Investment capital ruled over producers and consumers. "They adorn us with prices that keep us more naked than adorned" was a quip in Nicaragua in 1786. The Intendant of San Salvador did not hesitate to remark in 1793 about the "tyranny of Guatemala City over the Provinces." Quotes such as these abound.

The indigo trade's high point also had other notable consequences. It united all the growers along the Pacific strip from the south of Guatemala to the Nicoya Peninsula as a business activity. Indigo and the commercial cattle industry competed with and in many cases replaced subsistence agriculture. This reinforced their business character. But, it also promoted a labor shortage and caused a rise in the price of food. The growing population of mestizo laborers was noticeable throughout this area even as early as the 1770s. A century later their growth would definitively push aside the Indian settlements and their communal property ownership. Local creole landowners (hacendados criollos) faced the realities of international economy, usurious credit, speculators in Guatemala and Cádiz (Spain), as well as the pressure and expectations of the colonial bureaucracy, and they began to see their own interests separately from those of the monarchy and other social groups. Conflicts and events began to transform them gradually into their own class. Their reality contrasted starkly with that of Guatemala. In the latter the bureaucrats, big businessmen, and the Church dominated native communities, took full advantage of being at the center of power in the capital city and fattened themselves by being on the routes of overseas trade (Guatemala City–Gulf of Dulce or Guatemala City–Bay of Honduras) created by the natural dynamics of trading monopolies.

We must develop a proper appreciation of the Bourbon reforms to complete our picture of the transformations that took place in the eighteenth century. The new dynamics of the colonial state were now expressed through a peculiar mixture of delayed mercantilism and administrative centralism. This peculiarity was not really a new idea of absolutism that arose with the change of dynasty. Rather it was a reinvigorated view of effective state administration serving an imperial idea.

Centralism led to a struggle against many private privileges and rights, especially those of the old established families who had inherited the spoils of the first period of conquest and colonization. Sending new officials to the colonies was indispensable to at least the partial success of more far-reaching state control. The Church, which had been the true power under the Hapsburg dynasty, was notably affected by the inroads of secular control, although only to a limited degree.

Changes in administrative responsibilities were required to modernize colonial government grown decrepit over two hundred years. These changes favored local vested interests and in some cases even worked to create such interests. The changes affected the older pattern of regional privileges. The real motives behind this renewal of the colonial administration were crystal clear in theory and practice underneath the manifold diversity that the Bourbons revealed throughout the century: defense of the empire and greater income.

This new political economy enshrined in mature form the principles of mercantilism practiced during the seventeenth century by France, England, and Holland. It was, in this sense, really a delayed readjustment of the earlier less-developed mercantilism that held sway during the Hapsburg dynasty. Exclusive economic control over the colonies continued to be the foundation. This was managed by promoting chartered companies (until 1756) and a "liberalization" of trade between the Spanish colonies themselves, especially after 1778. Still the term "free trade" should not mislead us. In reality we are dealing with a less burdensome and more efficient monopoly designed to assure the greatest returns to the vested interests of the mother country, which were epitomized in the Crown and the major businessmen. An effort to promote the sale of manufactures produced in Spain by the state to supply the demands of a vast colonial market quickly fizzled. A modern, although delayed, response to these colonial market demands was the development of the textile industry during the latter half of the eighteenth century in Catalonia.

If we compare these Bourbon reforms in Central America with what was happening in other places, such as the River Plate region, Mexico, or Cuba, the changes seem hardly significant. The Kingdom of Guatemala continued to be marginal and on the periphery of the vast colonial complex. From inside Central America, however, our evaluation changes. The unspectacular transformation and its meager final outcome in regards to economic development stand in stark contrast to the acrimonious conflicts between the "provincials" and the "Guatemalans," not to mention the bitter and complex confrontations that occurred between the various levels of the social ladder.

Fiscal reorganization was a cornerstone of Bourbon policy. Commuting the assessed tribute in 1747 forced native communities to be incorporated into the mercantile economy at the same time as tributes diminished as a revenue source for state coffers: from 73 percent of total collected revenue between 1694 and 1698 to 37 percent between 1771 and 1775 to only 18 percent between 1805 and 1809.

New revenue sources were acquired from the monopolies on liquor (1758) and tobacco (1765). Additionally the monopolies on gunpowder and playing cards were moved from Mexico to Guatemala. Raising the *alcabala* (sales tax) and the *Barlovento* (port tax) as well as more secure controls in their collection completed the fiscal reform scheme. By the period 1805–1809 income from these monopolies and the *alcabala* provided over 80 percent of state revenue. A century earlier a similar proportion of state income had been derived from Indian tributes.

This important shift in the fiscal structure ought not to be understood as magnanimity in the face of the exploitation that the native communities suffered. Change in tributes and the forced monetarization of their economy placed the Indians in the clutches of traders and speculators. At the same time, since 1776, income from the native communities had become managed by judges and administrative officials (alcaldes mayores). The efficacy of these changes can be clearly seen through the eyes of the colonial state. These new and important resources were directed toward bettering defense and the economic infrastructure. Sending income from Central America to Spain had never figured as a priority under Bourbon policy. This was a major shift from the attitude of the Hapsburg dynasty in the seventeenth century. This greater flexibility and margin generated material support for the struggle against the English along the Atlantic Coast and for revitalizing trade activity.

Indian uprisings continued to be the standard response to colonial exploitation. Even though it is difficult to be certain if, given the administrative changes mentioned, there was an increase in Indian unrest, certain signs do point in this direction. The main triggers for uprisings were the manifold abuses by royal officials, but there were also rebellions against changes in the system of tributes and methods by which they were collected. There was a wave of these rebellions toward the end of the colonial period. The *Ordenanza de Intendentes* (Statute Regarding Revenue Officers) of 1806 attempted to equalize the burden of the tributes, but the Parliament of Cádiz abolished tributes in 1811. Ferdinand VII reestablished tributes in 1815. We must wait until the Liberal revolution of 1820 and the restoration of the 1812 Constitution to witness their abolition.

Spanish efforts to dislodge the English completely from Belize fell short each time, but Great Britain was forced to recognize Spanish sovereignty on various occasions, as for example: the Treaty of Paris (1763) that ended the Seven

Years' War, the Peace of Paris (1783) concluding the independence of the United States, and the London Convention (1786). In each of the three, the English were permitted to log where, in practice even if illegally, a hundred years of occupation had made unquestionably their territory. The Spanish presence in the Bay of Honduras was asserted when the Omoa fortifications were built in 1756 and reached its peak when Trujillo was repopulated in 1780. Although the English efforts to wrest control of the San Juan River failed in 1780 with their taking and subsequent retreat from Fort Immaculada, so too had the Spanish failed to remove British influence from Mosquitia. In summary, even though the Spanish did not enjoy complete success in their struggles against the English, at least they prevented the English settlements simply annexing the whole Atlantic Coast. Tradewise, we should note another modest success: between 1760 and 1790 smuggling diminished and Spanish fleets frequently plied the waters of the Bay of Honduras.

The "free trade" decreed in 1778 seemed to bring with it few direct benefits to the Kingdom of Guatemala. There was neither a sizeable increase in the movement of products nor any new incentives to stimulate future production in the long range.

The Ordenanza de Intendente of 1785 reorganized the administrative structure of the colony by creating separate governments for San Salvador, Chiapas, Honduras, and Nicaragua (which included Costa Rica) in a seeming effort to decentralize. Guatemala City's importance declined and local interests gained increasing power (especially in El Salvador). Still it was setting up the Consulado de Comercio de Guatemala in 1793 that provided a rather harsh antidote, since it underscored the power of monopolistic traders and financiers in the capital allied with the merchants of Cádiz.

The decade of the 1790s saw a crisis of general proportions whose impact was felt for several decades. On one side, the war in Europe ended with Spanish defeats, guaranteeing the undisputed English preeminence over the Atlantic. The Bourbon dynasty collapsed in 1808. The independence of

Spain itself was in question when the French invaded and, as we well know, this collapse of Spanish power occurred only a few short years before the independence of the Spanish American colonies. The recession may have anticipated the war with England of 1798, but in any case it was worsened by the lack of safe trade routes. The indigo crisis reflects a decline in the quality of the product, competition from other producing areas, and new plagues of locusts (1802-1803). On top of all this was the collapse of the state itself. Between 1780 and 1800 military expenditures vastly exceeded the fiscal resources of the Kingdom of Guatemala. Between 1805 and 1809 the situation became even worse. Miles Wortman sees the situation as an "overextension of fiscal resources for bureaucratic and defensive purposes, which, when retrenched because of a decline in fiscal income, led to a collapse in central authority." The exhausted administration slowly lost all ability to mediate the angry conflicts between the "provincials" and Guatemala City. Loss of trade forced the government to allow trade with neutral countries in 1797 and to close its eyes to increased smuggling. From that point on, Belize came to play a key role that was strengthened by war and crisis in the mother country.

Severe recession and the erosion in state authority became permanent during the first two decades of the nineteenth century. There seemed no way out of the crisis. This was clearly reflected in the attitudes of the criollo provincial elite. In Mexico and South America, patriots were waging a life and death struggle for independence. Fear of this prompted a brief utopian period of constitutionalism in Cádiz (1812). This highpoint of Spanish Enlightenment, implying a new sort of alliance with the colonies based on liberal principles, was stillborn. Restoration of absolutism in 1814 in Spain not only burst this dream but also meant prison and persecution for Central American liberals themselves. Independence came finally more as a result of outside pressures than from efforts by domestic classes or local groups. Events in Mexico in 1821 provided the key link to what was inevitable. When

Agustín de Iturbide ended the popular insurrection for independence, he invited the Central American authorities to adopt the principles of the Plan of Iguala. These were independence (from Spain), Catholicism, and unification of Mexico and Spain under a constitutional monarchy. Politically speaking, September 15, 1821, incarnated a true "revolution from above."

We must take note of certain shifts in vested interests that had occurred in the preceding years. The colonial bureaucracy had become as irrelevant as the fictitious relationship between Guatemala and Cádiz. The wealthiest members of the Consulado now stridently held aloft the banner of free trade (with England) in Guatemala City. Their motives were simple. Since 1818 they had restored their preeminence and replaced their Spanish trading partners in Cádiz with English ones in Belize. A stereotypical example of this can be found in the Aycinena family, which juggled its financial interests and family connections between Spain and the local criollos to achieve the shift. This transformation kept intact the rule of trade financiers as it had been twenty years earlier.

Under these conditions, by 1821, the key problem for the "provincials" continued to be to rupture the hated monopoly of trade. The authority of colonial governments was exhausted and had by then entirely crumbled. Next there were outbreaks of other conflicts no less deeply rooted, such as the opposition between cities and regions: the provinces of Granada and León [in Nicaragua], the cities of Tegucigalpa and Comayagua [in Honduras], the cities of Cartago and San José [in Costa Rica], and the cities of Guatemala and Quezaltenango [in Guatemala].

No one has better expressed what independence signified than the Honduran scholar José Cecilio del Valle. On November 30, 1821, he wrote these words in his gazette *El Amigo de la Patria* (Friend of the Nation):

> The new world shall not be in the future, what it has been hitherto, a sad tributary of the old world. The American shall labor to increase his personal productive wealth: he will labor

to provide to the Government, protector of his rights, the necessary income for maintaining order. But he shall not crawl about caverns in the earth to extract from its bosom metals to be sent to another continent.

America shall not lag a century behind Europe: it will stride as an equal first, and lead later; it will, in the end, be the most illuminated by the sciences just as it is most illumined by the sun. . . . There shall arise learned among our assimilated natives [ladinos] and philosophers among our Indians: all shall partake to a greater or lesser degree of civilization. . . . The ones shall not trample upon the rights of the others: men shall show respect for themselves in showing it toward their peers: and morality, which is mutual respect for the rights of all, shall shine forth in these lands where it has been darkest.

These sublime reflections, however, close with a warning that would prove a bitter truth in the coming years:

But to reach that pinnacle of power it will be necessary to climb rugged heights, to go down perilous trails, to cross over abysses. Let us not conceal the risks of our position. Let us broadcast the truth so that its knowledge may make us prudent.

## 3

# In Search of Progress: Independence and the Formation of Nation-States in the Nineteenth Century

### THE FAILURE OF THE CENTRAL AMERICAN FEDERATION

The annexation to Mexico was short-lived. Problems inherent in a power center too far removed were added to difficulties in reconciling manifold local interests. Ambitions for autonomy in Quezaltenango, Tegucigalpa [Honduras] and Costa Rica crossed over into more traditional jealousies of the "provincials" vis-à-vis Guatemala. Meanwhile the Salvadoreans did not hide their open republicanism. Almost everyone hoped that annexation would provide a solution to interminable administrative conflicts and an end to an overly prolonged economic backwardness. During 1822 it became increasingly clear that those were only dreams.

Iturbide sent a force of 600 men under the command of Vicente Filísola, a Neapolitan brigadier general with great political acumen, to be headquartered in Guatemala City with the mission of preserving peace and order. Soon, however, the Mexicans were viewed as crude invaders. The Salvadorean republicans had never accepted the annexation agreement of January 1822 and from December of 1821 had tried to win backing from the other provinces. Even though these efforts did not produce immediate results, events led to an open independence movement that climaxed in December of 1822 when El Salvador proclaimed its desire to unite with the United States of America. Mexican troops crushed the Salvadorean republicans in February 1823, but the victory was short-lived. At that very moment Iturbide (who had been emperor for six months) was overthrown by rebellious Mexican generals and the whole country was convulsed by civil war. Filísola's position could not have been weaker. Promised Mexican financial assistance had never come and expenses of maintaining the troops rested with the Guatemalan government. On March 29, Filísola chose to convene a congress (which had actually been provided for by the Declaration of Independence of September 15, 1821) to decide the issue of annexation.

On July 1, 1823, the congress met in Guatemala City and proclaimed Central America's complete independence. It then declared itself a General Constituent Assembly. A month later, Filísola withdrew with his troops. On the way back, he was able to seal Chiapas's union with Mexico and its final separation from the old Kingdom of Guatemala. Meanwhile, the delegates from Costa Rica, Nicaragua, and Honduras arrived and were seated retroactively in the Assembly where they ratified the declaration of July 1.

The interlude of annexation with Mexico was thus ended and the Central Americans now believed themselves masters of their own destiny. This, at least, shone through the fervor of the deputies at the Assembly when they grandly proclaimed the "United Provinces of Central America" to be a nation, "sovereign, free, and independent of old Spain, of Mexico, and of all other powers whether of the Old or the New World." This same thrust was reflected in all the labors of the Assembly, which climaxed its sessions on November 22, 1824, promulgating a Constitution. Under the banner of "God, Unity and Liberty," the representatives had chosen a federalist model of organization. The new republic, officially called "Federation of Central America," was constituted by five states: Guatemala, El Salvador, Honduras, Nicaragua, and Costa Rica.

The Constitution combined the influence of the U.S. Constitution and that of Cádiz (of 1812) with a generous dose of eighteenth-century enlightenment. Its authors, or those who inspired it (among whom we find the Honduran José Cecilio del Valle), displayed social imagination and a certain political

**Maps 9, 10.** These maps illustrate the final territorial configuration of the five Central American states, which came about slowly and through struggle.

On map 9, the state of Los Altos, separated from Guatemala in 1838–39, is shown. Costa Rica has already annexed the former *Alcaldía* of Nicoya (1824–25).

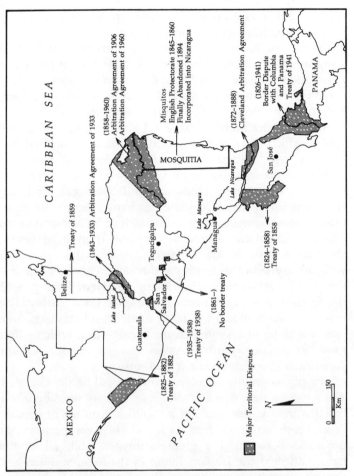

On map 10 border wars and the current political division are summarized. This map illustrates how slow and difficult it was to
settle frontiers, and the considerable number of disputes concerning the Nicaraguan Mosquitia and the Costa Rican Atlantic
coastal regions.

realism. But, was it possible to dress up the ancient body of Central American societies in new clothes?

On the one hand, material reasons conspired against creating any sort of federalism. Weakening proportional representation were the isolation of the different states, the poor communication between regions, and the unbalanced distribution of the population. Around 1824, the population of Central America scarcely exceeded 1 million, almost 50 percent of which was concentrated in Guatemala. The First Federal Congress, inaugurated in April of 1825, had, therefore, eighteen representatives from Guatemala, nine from El Salvador, six apiece from Honduras and Nicaragua, and only two from Costa Rica. On the other hand, there were structural economic weaknesses in the lack of income-producing exports without any alternatives in view. Then there was the showdown between the Guatemalans and the provincials with the myriad of jealousies and resentments built up over the years that were far from being resolved. Finally, with the Spanish retreat, the British presence grew visibly. This was particularly evident in trade matters and strategic interests (the issue of an interoceanic canal), all of which subtly came to ensnare Central America, even making Central Americans take sides against each other.

The physiognomy of colonial society had hardly changed. The mestizos now had a greater role. Slavery was abolished, but this in any case was not a significant means of production. There was now free trade. These were perhaps the innovations having the greatest impact. Still, all of this hardly affected the Indians living in their communities and the poor mestizos living on their *rancherías* (subsistence farms) near large haciendas and the cities. Even for the large landowners and cattle ranchers living in the undeveloped interior of the Isthmus things were not much changed.

At its heart, there was an insoluble antinomy between the zealous independence of the individual states and the very possibility of federal power itself. Two situations arose in 1823–1824, a period of discussion and hope like none that had come before, which well illustrate the crippling effect of these contradictions.

The imbalance between the various states required some territorial adjustments. They were easily reachable only in the case of the Administrative–Judicial Region (Alcaldía Mayor) of Sonsonate, incorporated into El Salvador in November 1823, and that of Nicoya, annexed to Costa Rica in July 1824. The matter of the State of Los Altos, in comparison, was much thornier. The districts (comarcas) of the Guatemalan highlands (Quezaltenango, Suchitepéquez, Sololá, and Totonicapán) comprised 129 villages and over 200,000 inhabitants. These were more than sufficient in resources to create a sixth state in the Federation. In fact, promises and discussions along these lines date from 1823. There were, however, active opposing interests between Quezaltenango and Guatemala City. It is equally apparent that had this sixth state been created it would have materially altered the sociopolitical balance of power in the Federation. It was this uncertainty that impelled the Conservatives and Liberals alike to delay its creation. When it was finally completed in 1838, the Federation was stillborn. The effect of the balance of powers was reduced to yet another step toward separatism.

The creation of new bishoprics was yet another chilly issue since it implied a recognition of autonomy even beyond religious matters (aside from economic issues, it had to do with control of the Royal Patronage (Patronato Real)). Facing Guatemalan opposition, the Salvadoreans opted for a fait accompli in creating their own bishopric in 1822, formally ratifying this decision two years later. Fray Matías Delgado, a leading Republican and an equally strong supporter of a Central American union, was elevated to bishop. Although the Vatican resisted such presumption, with the situation only being resolved in 1842, it reflects clearly how ambitions toward autonomy quickly led to the exercise of sovereign powers by member states. Costa Rica's efforts toward its own bishopric were firmly opposed by authorities in León and never reached such a point. There were other, equally disquieting signs, nonetheless. In 1823, the Costa Rican government negotiated an agreement with the cities of Granada and León in which territorial and commercial matters were included. This was yet another act that implied the exercise of full national sovereignty.

The Federal Republic had a brief and unsettled existence. The First Congress was convened in 1825 and elected as its president the Salvadorean liberal Manuel José Arce. Soon at odds with the Congress, Arce formed an alliance with Guatemalan Conservative groups and gave them free reign over the government of their state. Those resentments and quarrels that had seethed somewhat peacefully from 1821 through 1825 now broke forth violently. The Conservative Guatemalans entered into a close alliance with the Church and became alarmed at the radical reformism of the Liberals. The latter for their part saw in all this another attempt by the partisans of Guatemalan hegemony to restore its supremacy and trample the Constitution. The Civil War ended in 1829 with a triumph of the Liberal band under the leadership of the Honduran Francisco Morazán. The outlook could not have been grimmer. Calamities and destruction were heaped onto an already weakened economy.

Arce had negotiated a loan to the Federation from the London banking house of Barclay, Herring and Richardson in 1825. Of the 5 million pesos loaned, slightly over 300,000 actually entered the treasury, and this was soon consumed by the war. This enormous debt was yet another legacy of the war. It gave the English Consul Chatfield sufficient basis to be menacing in demands for repayment that combined with open English territorial ambitions along the Atlantic Coast.

The Conservative reaction was embodied particularly by the Guatemalan Church hierarchy and the large traders in the capital city and promised to become a fierce resistance to any efforts at radical change. Finally, the various states during the years of civil war had assumed independence in legal matters and in those involving treasury and finance.

The Liberals, militarily triumphant, reconvened Congress in 1829 and resolved to proceed with energy. They expelled the archbishop of Guatemala, expropriated the holdings of the religious orders, and hounded the most prominent Conservatives. Morazán was elected president in 1830 and resolved to restore the authority of the federal government. The question remained: how could this be achieved without adequate income and under an ambiguous Constitution? In practical terms, federal authority could only increase at the cost of that of the individual states. In 1835 several reforms were proposed for the Constitution which were never enacted and when, in 1838, Congress resolved to turn over to the federal government control of the customs income, which was the only way to assure federal finances, the union disintegrated. Nicaragua first, and later Costa Rica and Honduras, decided to secede.

Mariano Gálvez, chief of state in Guatemala from 1831 to 1838, tried to implement a wide-ranging program of Liberal reforms. These centered on free trade, developing exports, some protectionism regarding the textile industry, freedom of religion, universal education, judicial reforms, and a colonization program. His efforts, however, only stimulated conflict with the Indian communities and frequent confrontations with the Church. There were growing disagreements within Liberal ranks, moreover, not to mention the impasse Morazán faced as president in achieving true power for the federal government.

Export of indigo and cochineal picked up in the early 1830s while the protection of the textile industry promised to restore its earlier prominence that had been undercut by British imports. All this turned out to be a temporary illusion. Shortages of cash and rising interest rates conspired with the enormous debt. The colonization project in Petén, Chiquimula, Verapaz, and Totonicapán began with three major concessions that immediately provoked strong reactions among the Indians of Chiquimula, who rose up in arms in 1835, and it also increased hostility toward foreigners throughout the country.

Freedom of religion incited strong Church opposition. In addition the government never could assume control of the Civil Registry, and the hospitals and schools that it took over faced enormous problems. The major judicial reform was the introduction of the legal codes as written by Edward Livingston for Louisiana in 1826. These codes were viewed as anticlerical and an instance of foreign interference. The attempts to establish trial by jury in El Salvador (1832), and in Nicaragua and Guatemala (1835), represented very utopian efforts in a society the majority of whose population was illiterate and dominated ideologically by the Church.

Nothing inspired greater reaction than taxation. Indian tributes had been abolished in 1811, later restored, and then finally abolished again with Independence. Gálvez restored them in 1831. He imposed "direct taxation" on mestizo peasants and artisans with the tithe being replaced in 1832 by a land tax of four reals for each *caballería*.[1] An 1836 decree combined all these taxes and seems to have been the immediate cause for a general Indian uprising in 1837 headed by Rafael Carrera. We should not, however, lose sight of a general restlessness that was already manifest in various ways. In 1832 and 1833, El Salvador was shaken by Indian uprisings in San Vicente and Tejutla. Discontent was also quite apparent in Honduras and Nicaragua. We should point out that on the whole the Liberal reforms did not insure any immediate improvement, but they did follow hard upon a period of destruction, forced taxation, and general disorder.

Even though Morazán had moved the federal capital to San Salvador in 1834, the same year he was reelected president by Congress, his Federation's fortunes followed events in Guatemala. At the beginning of 1837 a terrible epidemic of cholera (colera morbus) broke out that ravaged the more heavily populated regions of the Guatemalan high plains. The government quarantined certain areas and undertook several preventative measures; however, the village priests declared that it was divine punishment and spread the rumor that government officials were poisoning the water.

Panic and violence among mestizos and Indians were the result in the high plains. There were two reasons why the insurrection did not simply become a series of rural outbursts. Rafael Carrera, former mestizo pig farmer, revealed in the Mita hills outstanding abilities as a leader in guerrilla warfare. The second reason was that the Church and the Conservatives were able to gain control and to manipulate the insurrection politically.

Gálvez left the government at the end of 1837. From that point to the time when Carrera defeated Morazán in March of 1840 is one of the most complicated and confusing episodes in Central American history. In 1838 the Federal Republic was reeling from the secession of the various states, threats from the English, and Conservative reaction in Honduras, Nicaragua, and Guatemala. In February 1839 when Morazán's term of office concluded, Congress dissolved and there was no legal body to name his successor. Through the rest of that year, the various forces maneuvered and aligned themselves for the final showdown. This took place in March of 1840. In point of fact, from February of 1839 onward the Federation was a thing of the past. In 1842 Morazán attempted to return to Central America to continue the struggle toward unification; however, this venture ended tragically for him. On the fifteenth of September in 1842 he fell before a firing squad in San José, Costa Rica.

The disintegration of the Central American Federation and the first Liberal regime had long-lasting consequences for the Isthmus. Gálvez's ambitious program in Guatemala had tried to put an end to three basic traits of colonial society: (1) the Church's political, ideological, and economic influence; (2) the ancient division between the "Indian Republic" and the "Hispanic Republic"; and (3) the isolation and weakness of the region's incorporation into world markets. Carrera's triumph and the Conservative restoration halfway through the nineteenth century mortgaged, in a sense, the future of Central America. The Liberal upsurge during the 1870s reduced the Church's power and also achieved a successful integration into world markets. Displaying skillful pragmatism the new Liberals put the Indian question to the side for the time being.

Outside of Guatemala itself, the Liberal programs were more moderate in character although they still aroused some antagonisms. These, however, responded entirely to local interests. In Honduras the conflict between Tegucigalpa and Comayagua threatened to divide the country into two states; but in 1823 the two agreed to alternate the capital from one city to the other annually. Although in subsequent years things were not quite so simple, much less peaceful, during the 1830s a modus vivendi was attained that lasted to the close of the century: the capital remained in Comayagua but administration officials often resided in Tegucigalpa, a city that continued to grow in population and economic power. In Nicaragua, the antagonisms were even more pronounced. Liberalism seemed to have flourished in León while the Conservatives ruled in Granada. Their struggle gave no quarter and the country was plunged for years into anarchy. Morazán sent the Honduran Dionisio de Herrera who achieved a temporary peace between 1830 and 1833 during which time he was able to consolidate Liberal power. This power reached its highest expression in the 1838 Constitution. Paradoxically it was the same Congress that ratified the Constitution, in Chinandega, that also voted for the secession of Nicaragua from the Central American Federation and thereby contributed in a major way to the Liberal defeats in Guatemala and El Salvador.

Costa Rica's development in the south of the Isthmus had some peculiarities all its own. With its tiny population (only about 50,000 around 1800) and rather isolated from the rest of Central America, the colonial legacy had come down as one of peasant farmers who were jealous of their independence and dedicated to subsistence farming. A brief surge in tobacco exports toward the close of the colonial period barely altered the existing social order, but it did provide a valuable lesson in management for farmers and businessmen. This lesson was taken advantage of in the 1830s when

Costa Rica began to export coffee to England. This is a particularly important event since it is the first definite step toward a new period in Central American history. Blessed with its geographical isolation, Costa Rica did not become embroiled in any of the Federation's internal strife. Braulio Carrillo, who was the head of state between 1835 and 1842, created the organizational framework for the new nation. His handiwork was developed gradually throughout the subsequent decades. In Costa Rica, distinctions between Liberals and Conservatives were much less marked than for the rest of Central America. This situation is no doubt due to the fact that early successes in exporting coffee unified the socioeconomic foundation of Costa Rican society.

Strife brought down the Federation. The conflicts between Liberals and Conservatives are very easily sketched in an ideological framework. The Liberals believed in a utopia of progress: to bring forth to these lands soaked with obscurantism and backwardness the flame lit by the French Revolution and the independence of the United States. In short, to hitch the future to the chariot of "Prometheus Unbound." The Conservatives longed for the colonial way of life. They had boundless respect for the Church and they feared any social change they could not control. In a nutshell, we are dealing with enlightened despotism. As is always the case, the clearness of the ideas contrasted with personal ambitions, political opportunism, unplanned events, and the complex underpinning of the vested interests in play.

The opposition between Guatemalans and the provincials had always been present historically and had as its principal theater Guatemala, Honduras, and El Salvador. Besides this opposition were local ones between cities and the surrounding regions. The loyalties and limits between one party and the other were consequently fluid and often disconcerting. One could argue that opportunism ruled during this period more than in others or that some leaders lacked the required judgment or imagination. No doubt these traits were very evident during those tumultuous years. But all this apparent chaos, this hopeless tragic destiny, was perhaps also secretly ruled by the vast difference between the Liberal political programs and social reality.

The role of foreign influence in the fall of the Federation is still debated. Let us observe first that even such factors, whose influence could be supposed to be immediately positive—as for example, the colonial development of agriculture and immigration—were a complete failure. The 1825 loan was a disgrace and the interoceanic canal issue only awakened imperialist appetites. The British consul, Frederick Chatfield, had a particularly active diplomatic role in any case. Liberal historiography has traditionally attributed to him the major blame for the "balkanization" of the Isthmus. Mario Rodríguez, however, has persuasively demonstrated that only after the 1838 crisis did Chatfield become a "formidable enemy" of the Central American union. We should not lose sight of the fact that the territorial ambitions of the English along Central America's Atlantic Coast were constant both before and after the events in question. The return in 1816 to the old custom of "crowning" a "king" of Mosquitia is consistent with the declaration of a protectorate over that zone in 1843.

After 1839 the concept of a united Central America had become a powerfully appealing utopia. For some it was an inspiring ideal while for others it was a pretext for the meddling of neighboring states in the affairs of one another; yet this dream has remained a constant presence up to the present day.

## CONSERVATIVE RESTORATION AND
## FOREIGN THREATS

Separatism ruled during the 1840s. The Church recovered its power in Guatemala, and Carrera ruled with an iron hand until he died in 1865. He derived his support from the clergy, major merchants, and the Indians. The power of the Conservatives, however, was built up much more slowly than has been usually supposed. Initially Carrera only retained military power, having had the prudence to install in

Honduras and El Salvador two loyal strong men, Francisco Ferrera and Francisco Malespín. This expedient not only served to protect him from any possible Morazán reaction, it also provided him sufficient time to consolidate his complete control over Guatemala. In 1844 the Assembly named him "Worthy Leader and General in Chief" (Benemérito Caudillo y General en Jefe) as it handed him the presidency on the eleventh of December. Until his death in 1865 and save a brief lapse between 1848 and 1849, he exercised total and undisputed power.

The cochineal cultivated in the environs of Guatemala City and so prized in Europe as a source of red dye provided the basis in the 1850s for a moderate prosperity that had the virtue of not requiring radical changes in transportation methods (mules and Indian porters) or in the financial system (monopolized by the Church and major merchants). The minimal need for labor also assured some peace in the Indian communities. Additionally, Carrera reached a generous agreement with British interests in 1859 in which he recognized their occupation of Belize in exchange for the building of a road between Guatemala City and the Caribbean coast.

The perpetuation of the colonial structure was also visible in El Salvador. Indigo exports revived, and this was the primary trade product until the 1880s. Coffee also started to be cultivated beginning in 1846. The production system used for indigo resembled that for cochineal. Small- and medium-scale mestizo producers (poquiteros) received advances from urban traders who in turn took care of export markets. The larger plantations made use of laborers from the Indian communities and Castilianized Indians (Ladinos). Even after the Federal Republic had disintegrated there seemed to remain some important ties between Salvadorean indigo merchants and the major traders in Guatemala City. Even though demand for dye was clearly increasing during the middle of the nineteenth century, there soon appeared clouds on the horizon: other countries were beginning to compete and, more importantly, synthetic dyes were becoming available.

Honduras exhibited a similar regional disintegration and dispersion among the population centers. This situation had become notorious during the colonial period. Mining was only barely increasing in activity. Along the north coast, the English controlled logging and often brought laborers from Belize. Cattle from Olancho were being sold in Guatemala or in the San Miguel fairs of El Salvador. In each case the overland route the cattle took was long and difficult. Tegucigalpa itself was a declining mining center and hard to get to. Choluteca and Nacaome in the Gulf of Fonseca had become a necessary stage in the old overland route to the Pacific.

Nicaragua continued as the supplier of cattle for Central America, its role also in the colonial period. A relative surge in mining (in the Department of Chontales) and an incipient development of coffee production in the region surrounding Managua did not negate the archaic and primitive character of most economic activity. Indigo and cocoa continued to have some importance, especially in Rivas and Granada. The shortage of labor and the destruction occasioned by the continuing civil wars decidedly conspired against developing a plantation-style agriculture and reinforced the traditional preference for cattle ranching. Credit, in the hands of merchants in Granada, was rather usurious and typical of early merchant capitalism. It does not surprise us in these conditions that regionalism predominated everywhere.

The rapid expansion of the coffee trade in Costa Rica in the 1830s and success with exports to England along the Pacific route around Cape Horn brought about new perspectives. There were improvements in transportation and a slow modernization of state administration, to the extent that there arose a strong process of agricultural colonization by peasant families in the Central Valley. Also, a handful of newly immigrated European traders and businessmen (English, French, and German) acquired an early importance in the coffee trade. In fact, Central America began to see itself as a major coffee exporter toward the middle of the nineteenth century.

The threats of foreign intervention heightened in the 1840s and 1850s. The English infiltration was carried out under the cover of demanding payment for the 1825 federal debt, proportionately underwritten by the constituent states. When in 1839 the Federal Republic collapsed, this debt became a pretext for intervention that in reality had ulterior motives: to consolidate the settlement in Belize and to control the Nicaraguan Mosquitia, which they declared to be a protectorate in 1843 with the ultimate goal of a future interoceanic canal. This muscular Victorian diplomacy, embodied in the aggressive maneuvering of the British Consul Chatfield and especially in the presence of gunships, soon collided with the expansionist interests of the United States. By the Clayton–Bulwer Treaty of 1850, the British government was forced to renounce unilateral control of an interoceanic canal and both governments agreed not to colonize any part of Central America. The immediate effect of this latter provision was actually rather theoretical. The English temporarily occupied the Bay Islands in the Gulf of Honduras in 1852 and did not relinquish Mosquitia until 1894.

The Gold Rush in California in 1848 radically changed the already turbulent Isthmus. Before the U.S. transcontinental railroad was opened in 1869, traveling from the east coast to California was fastest by sea and required either crossing the Isthmus through Nicaragua (using the San Juan River, Lake Nicaragua, and then overland from Granada to the Pacific Coast) or through Panama where since January 1855 the interoceanic railroad had been in operation. Between 1848 and 1868, some 68,000 travelers had crossed Nicaragua on their way to California while about 57,000 returned by the same route. This movement created a steamship line controlled by Cornelius Vanderbilt and reawakened the Nicaraguan economy. The region's strategic importance was underscored, and new voracious appetites were unleashed.

Under the well-known aegis of Rafael Carrera, the Conservatives ruled Central American politics. Various efforts by Liberals to restore the union, which were almost always motivated by pressures from the British, ended as complete flops. Doroteo Vasconcelos, a former Morazán lieutenant, had taken power in El Salvador. In January of 1851 he had exacted promises by Honduras and Nicaragua to form a union. By February of that same year, however, he was defeated by Carrera in the Battle of San José de Arada. Yet another episode took place in 1853 when Trinidad Cabañas, another former Morazán ally, took power in Honduras and revealed plans for a union. Carrera succeeded again and restored a "Conservative Peace." In 1854 the pope conferred the Order of Saint Gregory on Carrera and he was crowned President for Life of Guatemala. New and more serious influences were beginning to threaten the Isthmus, however.

In 1855 the Nicaraguan Liberals called upon a Tennessee adventurer named William Walker who in return for generous promises of land concessions equipped a mercenary force. Walker easily took over and quickly set up a phantom government in Nicaragua controlled in reality by the mercenaries. The U.S. State Department recognized it in May of 1856 to the considerable alarm of the other Central American countries and also of Great Britain. In reality, Walker was preparing to annex Nicaragua to the United States, a move backed by growing investment, weapons, and men drawn from the slave-owning South staffing his mercenary army. The Central American governments united together against Walker and an army commanded by the president of Costa Rica, Juan Rafael Mora, and equipped by the British finally succeeded in defeating the mercenaries in May of 1857 after a year-long struggle. This war has been aptly called the "National Campaign." It assured the independence of Central America, but it also signified the highpoint of Conservative power in the Isthmus.

Mora in Costa Rica was a loyal ally of Carrera. Santos Guardiola, nicknamed "the Butcher," had been installed by him as president of Honduras in 1856. After the Walker episode, the Nicaraguan Conservatives remained in power for over thirty years until 1893. Only Gerardo Barrios of El Salvador openly tried to defy the strongman. Some educational reforms (setting up Teachers' Schools), and economic reforms (promoting coffee growing) or perhaps the solemn return of Morazán's remains to El Salvador, signaled the beginning of friction. The crisis came to a head in 1861–1862 when Barrios tried to intervene in Honduras and started to impinge on the interests of the clergy. Carrera defeated him the following year and reinstalled Francisco Dueñas as president.

The thirty or so years during which the Conservatives held sway in Nicaragua offer a rare example of "progressive stability." Slow modernization and limited political participation were distinctive features of the regime. The executive power was strong but moderated, and it passed, avoiding reelection of officeholders, among the members of the most distinguished ranching families of Granada. Frutos Chamorro, one of the founding patricians, gave voice to its principles with exemplary clarity while he fought for the 1858 Constitution that would replace the Liberal one of 1838: the essence was to limit to the greatest extent possible the precious guarantees of individual liberties—something not to be defiled by conceding them to everyone equally—but Chamorro declared that "merit, virtue and property" earned liberty "without distinctions."

During the 1860s major changes were taking place. The Panama railway had created an improved outlook for exporting. The Pacific Coast ports had replaced the Atlantic ports as centers of trade. The latter development has particular importance since it opened up opportunities for coffee exporting. Costa Rica's successful example was imitated enthusiastically. Conditions progressively matured and made possible several of the Liberal's programs that they had tried fruitlessly to carry out during the Federation period.

## LIBERAL REFORMS: A NEW SOCIAL ORDER

The Liberal wave that swept over Central America during the 1870s adhered to the credo of the fathers of independence. It defined itself as the living flame of Morazán and

Barrundia. Not only had the international ambience and economic conditions changed. In addition, this new generation of Liberals was pragmatic and positivist. Fundamental structural changes sought to free up resources needed to develop an export economy, the benefits from which to be monopolized by a handful of landowners and businessmen. This explains the restructuring of landownership and legislation dealing with labor. This new structure also meant a substantial change in class relations. The Church was eliminated as a power. Local oligarchies had to submit to central government. Success or failure nationally in promoting foreign trade conditioned the forming and developing of a ruling class whose economic and political interests were more homogeneous, less fragmented, than previously.

Liberal successes were particularly conspicuous first in Guatemala and shortly thereafter in El Salvador. The revolution triumphed in 1871. It was soon dominated by the figure of Justo Rufino Barrios, a young moneyed leading coffee grower whose lands lay close to the Mexican frontier. Agrarian reform was quick and radical. Ecclesiastic lands were expropriated in 1873. The emphyteutic census was abolished in 1877; this census had conferred perpetual renter's rights to landholdings. Unused lands were sold and distributed: between 1871 and 1883, hectares of land amounting to 387,755 [958,143 acres] were sold. This created a land market based on private property in the region most suitable for coffee production, along the Pacific slopes and inland up to 1,400 meters' [4,500 feet] altitude. It is useful to note that the privatization of plantations did not affect the Indian communities in the highlands. This region was too high and cool for coffee production, with the exception of some zones in the Departments of Huehuetenango, Quiché, Verapaz, and Chiquimula. There was also special legislation dealing with laborers. An act known as the Regulations Governing Day Laborers was enacted in 1877. It revived the colonial system requiring communities to provide seasonal workers and it also regulated the "advances" (habilitaciones) in money that forceably assigned Indian laborers to a particular grower. All of this was buttressed by laws that suppressed vagrancy and by local political control. The highland Indian communities were thus transformed into a source of seasonal labor for the coffee plantations. This forced labor mobilization endured until the 1930s. About 8.5 percent of all the Indians were affected by this situation up to 1880. Day laborers, mestizos, and poor criollos, many of whom had become dispossessed of land by the abolition of the emphyteutic census, furnished a permanent workforce needed for the new export crop under a system known as the *colonato*. The landless peasant received a parcel of land within the plantation on which he could grow what was necessary for his family's subsistence. In exchange he was required to work without pay on the plantation a certain number of hours per day or a given number of days per week or month. The agreements were oral and the system was governed only by custom.

"Peace, education and prosperity" was the rallying cry of the reform movement. There were two respects in which this slogan acquired particular significance: in terms of fueling fierce anticlericalism and of promoting the push for construction and public services that increased coffee exporting demanded. Roads and ports were built and a major railway was begun to the Atlantic Coast, the ideal route (opened in 1908) in the absence of a Panama Canal (opened in 1914). Growing financial needs led to foreign loans, and soon the nation itself and local businessowners lost control of their banking, their export trade, and its financing.

Anticlericalism was not purely economic in character. The expropriation of lands was only an episode, although a crucial one, in a larger struggle. The Church was an obstacle in the evolution of modern education since, according to the Pavón legislation of 1852, elementary schools were supervised by parish priests. In addition, the identification of the Church with the Carrera regime was so close that the Liberals did not hesitate to regard the Church as a real obstacle to developing democratic institutions. The Barrios government took the position of eliminating all traditional special

rights (fueros) and privileges held by the Church and re-
serving for the state the administration of education and the
civil registry of births, marriages, and deaths. The education
program was characterized by the introduction of positivism,
the development of elementary schools, the creation of in-
stitutes of high school education in the main cities, and the
modernization of the University of San Carlos with an open
bias toward the Liberal professions. Expulsion of religious
orders and closing of convents and monasteries completed
the destruction of ecclesiastical power.

Justo Rufino Barrios ruled dictatorially between 1873 and
1879. These institutional reforms were already well consolidated by 1879 when he decided to convene a constituent
assembly, and they were synthesized in a brief, and frequently ambiguous, document that granted a broad margin
of discretion to the chief executive as well as constantly underscoring the secular and centralized character of the state.
The pristine Liberal credo enshrined in the 1879 Constitution
(in effect in Guatemala until 1945) was limited in application
to the landed classes who in turn were hardly interested in
the formalities of representative democracy. Barrios himself
was an authoritarian, temperamental, and strong-minded
ruler who was not disposed to see his personal power limited. This power, although absolute, was always threatened
by uprisings, intrigues, and conspiracies. In a famous letter
Lorenzo Montúfar, a distinguished liberal intellectual, con-
fessed the dilemmas that confronted the writers of the Constitution:

> The Assembly was convoked and I was a deputy and part of
> its Constitutional Commission. This Commission sensed that
> General Barrios was comparable to an African lion impossible
> to contain in a cage of silken threads, and so the effort was
> to create a very large constitutional cage with a vast portal
> so that the lion might enter and exit without destroying the
> threads. . . . The Constitution was decreed and experience
> has demonstrated the foresight of the 1879 legislators. Barrios
> does not obey the Constitution. The lion does not exit the
> cage through the vast portal. It pleases itself with destroying
> the silken threads.

In relations with his neighbors, Barrios displayed tactics very similar to those of Rafael Carrera: to consolidate Liberal power in Guatemala required friendly rulers in Honduras and El Salvador. But in 1885, his policies took a more radical tack. On February 28 he promulgated a decree announcing the Central American unification into a single republic, accompanied by the ardent proclamation that "divided and isolated we are nothing, united we can become something and united we shall be." At the same time he proclaimed himself to be the supreme military commander of the new nation. This proclamation was immediately rejected by El Salvador, Costa Rica, and Nicaragua, not to mention by Mexico and the United States. Barrios took to the battlefield and within a month invaded El Salvador. He died, however, in the Battle of Chalchuapa. Here closed a new and ephemeral unionist episode.

In El Salvador, the Liberal reform closely followed Guatemalan influence. Above all it was the work of President Rafael Zaldívar (1876–1885). In contrast with Guatemala, the Church had few large landholdings and the Indian communities and common lands (ejidos) of the towns included the land most suited for coffee growing. Land expropriation began in 1879, and it heightened with the legislation of 1881 and 1882 that eliminated common lands and communities (comunales). The outcome was that El Salvador was proletarianized more quickly than any other part of Central America. This was accompanied by a reduced number of landowners cornering the arable land. Coffee production expanded rapidly in this country that boasted of a more densely concentrated population. Railway construction, port modernization, and road improvements were facilitated by a large surplus labor pool, a smaller geographical area, and only relatively modest natural obstacles. Although Zaldívar firmly resisted Barrios in 1885, his regime did not outlive the war that year. Liberal groups sparked a rebellion captained by General Francisco Menéndez. Thus, there opened a period of authoritarian military regimes invariably changed by coups d'etat (in 1890, 1895, and 1898) and characterized by a positivist and pragmatic liberalism enshrined in the 1886 Constitution.

Honduras and Nicaragua experienced Liberal reforms that were frustrated or incomplete. In Honduras, Marco Aurelio Soto, a puppet of Barrios, took power in 1876 and set out to do what he could in a fragmented country with a small and dispersed population. The interoceanic railway planned to connect the Port of Cortés, in the Gulf of Honduras, with the Gulf of Fonseca was a monumental debacle. This was due to the corruption of succeeding governments and to costs much higher than foreseen. Lacking cheap transportation methods and having a particularly rugged geography, the development of coffee for export under the Soto government (1876–1883) was doomed. Soto himself poured his own dreams into the old fatal illusion of silver mining. There was little progress in that area in a period of abundant worldwide production. Foreign investment rapidly took over the mining industry mired in its very antiquated techniques and methods of transportation.

Luis Bográn continued the work of Soto between 1883 and 1891, but his rise to power initiated a period of significant political instability that only ceased in 1894 with Policarpo Bonilla's ascent to office, firmly supported by the Nicaraguan Liberals. Bonilla's government lasted until 1899 and extended the Soto–Bográn program of institutional reforms and material progress. Still, the end results were meager. Regional fragmentation, enormous difficulties in communication between regions, and backwardness continued to dominate Honduran life and to prevent a truly national power from consolidating. For these reasons the pull of neighboring states was all to frequent and itself became a powerful element in the complex formula of Honduras's instability.

In Nicaragua we find an example of a liberal revolution that was late in coming and frustrated in its course. After Walker was defeated, there followed over thirty years of Conservative stability under the strong hegemony of the Granadan ranchers and merchants. In the 1880s a railway was built connecting Corinto and Momotombo. This line was extended many years later to connect up with Managua and Granada. Coffee cultivation spread along the western slopes lying between the Pacific Coast and the Lake Managua basin. Labor shortages constituted a major obstacle, however, that Conservative governments were never able to resolve in spite of laws against vagrancy (1881 and 1883) and various measures that transferred communal lands to private hands.

The Liberals came to power in 1893 under the leadership of José Santos Zelaya, a strongman who had much in common with Justo Rufino Barrios. His efforts to modernize Nicaragua were particularly important. They occurred in an authoritarian but very dynamic style of government. Railway construction continued apace with branches from León to Corinto, from Chinandega to El Viejo, and from Masaya to Diriamba. There were also plans to open lines toward the mountains of Matagalpa and Mosquitia. Foreign investment was strongly promoted, and there was a relative upsurge in mining. But the most significant event was the arrival of some businessmen dedicated to growing coffee. Zelaya was very helpful with facilities to provide for laborers, authorizing a system of private recruiting by agents (enganches), and indebtedness quite similar to indenture that was complemented by forced recruitment of vagrants and the jobless for the army. Within Nicaragua, coffee growing did not displace cattle ranching, which had been traditionally tied to Central American markets. Foreign investment in mining and various other extractive enterprises along the Atlantic Coast enjoyed a modest surge. This fragmentation of vested interests thus conspired decisively against the unity of the ruling class.

The issue of an interoceanic canal and foreign pressures (stronger than for any other country in the Isthmus) continued to weave ever-more complex patterns in a society already complex to begin with. The outcome surfaced with all its hesitations, retreats, contradictions, and dramatic fluidity in the U.S. intervention of 1912. The Marines arrived, determined to remain.

Zelaya, however, revealed unusual dynamism and audacity. In 1894 he regained control of Mosquitia and withstood English hostilities during the blockade of Corinto in 1895. He was a tough nut to crack for the U.S. interests trying to negotiate a canal treaty. The agreement proposed in 1901 was rejected by the U.S. State Department because it omitted extraterritorial rights. When rights to canal construction were ceded to a French company in 1902 and Panama achieved independence in 1903, interest in the canal moved south. The whole region had now become vital to U.S. economic and military interests, however.

There were institutional changes in the 1894 Constitution, called the "most liberal constitution," as well as in an important process of codification. But, the 1905 Constitution significantly reduced individual rights and guarantees and notably strengthened executive power. In fact and in law, Zelaya's regime returned to authoritarian methods.

Under the banner of union, Zelaya repeatedly intervened in Honduras and El Salvador. In the end, he got both nations to acquiesce and, together with Nicaragua, they formed the Grand Republic of Central America (República Mayor de Centroamérica). But these efforts went no further than the agreement stage, and the brief pact lasted only from 1895 to 1898. Yet another "unionist" attempt by Zelaya, between 1902 and 1907, led to a serious confrontation with Estrada Cabrera, absolute ruler of Guatemala. These efforts did not fail to arouse concern in Mexico and the United States. In a much more intricate panorama, the earlier schemes of Barrios in 1885 to unify the region by force were repeated. In fact, the insistence on unionism after the fall of the Federation in 1839 invariably took on three forms: (1) a collective defense against outside aggression (the war against Walker or support for Zelaya in 1895, for example); (2) a legitimizing pretext for interventions in the affairs of neighboring states (such as Barrios did in 1885 or Zelaya in 1895–1898 and 1902 and 1907); or (3) as a utopia devised by intellectuals (such as the Central American Unionist Party formed by Salvador Mendieta in 1899).

Zelaya was overthrown in 1909 by a Conservative plot while he was in the middle of a diplomatic struggle with the United States. The roots of this struggle included cancellation of concessions granted to U.S. companies and a variety of efforts by Zelaya to interest other world powers in the construction of a canal through Nicaragua, thereby introducing competition (and a threat) to the United States's Panamanian enterprise.

In Costa Rica, Liberalism imposed itself gradually. The reason, as we have already observed, was that coffee enjoyed early success in a society that had been isolated and had no "colonial heritage," that is, Costa Rica had a sparse population, lots of available land, and lacked coercive labor. Braulio Carrillo's efforts were built upon in succeeding decades. We should particularly mention President Castro Madriz's (1847–1849 and 1866–1869) promotion of public schooling and freedom of the press. General Tomás Guardia's (1870–1882) dictatorship offers a rare example of "progressive authoritarianism": he promulgated the 1871 Constitution that was in force until 1949 (except between 1917 and 1919), and he abolished the death penalty and undertook an ambitious modernization program with broad participation of foreign investors. The latter included such projects as a railway construction contract to the Atlantic Coast, the equipping of Port Limón, and so forth. His successors, Próspero Fernández and Bernardo Soto, abolished the special privileges enjoyed by the clergy and pushed through a drastic reform in the educational system. Still, the Liberal watershed during the last quarter of the nineteenth century is less one of major restructuring than of consolidating social control achieved by means of a legal framework that allowed for exercising political power along with political participation. The acid test came in 1889 when the Liberals accepted their electoral defeat. The regimes of José Joaquín Rodríguez (1890–1894) and Rafael Yglesias (1894–1902) were authoritarian in character, but they did continue modernization programs although the economic climate was particularly adverse.

The electoral campaigns of 1901 and 1905–1906 were not clean ones, yet the political campaign style was closer to a working representative democracy. There was much less focus on the charisma and connections of the candidates (personalismo) than was true in the other Central American countries. Compromise was becoming ever more accepted as a rule of the political game in Costa Rica, and there was relative respect for the legal framework and for freedom of the press. All this led in subsequent decades to the gradual successful incorporation of new sectors of society into the political process.

## STATE, SOCIETY, NATION

To render judgment of the past from the vantage point of the present can be unfair, not to mention arbitrary. Still, it is necessary to evaluate somehow the path taken from Independence through the end of the last century. Let us weigh matters on the basis of three fundamental processes: (1) the triumph of separatism; (2) the consolidation of the nation-states; and (3) the transformation of Liberal ideology, from romantic utopia into positivist pragmatism.

Separatism progressively took over throughout the century. The Central American Federation fell apart amidst a general civil war. Subsequent efforts to revive it in the decades of 1840 to 1860 shared the same fate: wars, destruction, and death. Justo Rufino Barrios and José Santos Zelaya, in the final quarter of the nineteenth century, did not have any better luck. Rather, they promoted new internecine conflicts in an already quite stormy atmosphere.

The triumph of separatism paralleled the consolidation of the nation-states. The earliest unmistakable signs are visible at the very moment of independence: in each major city the elites who wielded power began to act with an overweening and all too arrogant autonomy. The next stage appeared during the ephemeral Mexican annexation and the various mutations of the Federal Republic: the issue of choosing a national capital. Wherever there was no urban center whose supremacy was unquestioned, such as with Honduras, Nicaragua, and Costa Rica, the building of a power center of national proportions implied both that the urban hierarchies would be simplified and that local interests would become subordinated to a central administration. This came about sooner (Costa Rica) or later (Honduras and Nicaragua).

The consolidation of state power depended on three classes of factors. First, the colonial past promoted certain territorial units and hindered others. Second, there were special historical opportunities and circumstances. Most of these were seen during the civil wars of the federalist period; foreign interventions need to be counted as well. There were three "negative" examples that help us appreciate these key moments. Chiapas seceded from the former Kingdom of Guatemala with the help of Mexico opportunely provided by Filísola's troops. The state of Los Altos had an ephemeral existence whereas Belize ended up consolidated into an English colonial enclave. Costa Rica's geographical isolation decidedly favored its early formation into a nation-state. The structuring of the nation-states depended on a third class of factors. These were the dynamic interactions between the development of state power and expansion of an agricultural export economy.

It was difficult to replace those sectors of the colonial economy that had been progressively disintegrating since the close of the eighteenth century. When real alternatives did appear after independence, they came with exasperating delay. New initiatives were difficult to carry out when there were long-standing vested interests that only reluctantly abandoned the old colonial ways. By the middle of the nineteenth century, the contrast between the early success of Costa Rican coffee production and the renewal of the old options in the other states of Honduras, El Salvador, Guatemala, and Nicaragua is symptomatic. In the Costa Rican case, coffee production grew thanks to a favorable combination of events and a strong effort by a handful of visionary traders. Within Costa Rica, they did not face serious opposition. In the other countries, by contrast, too much risk or lack of new opportunities led to reorganizing or reestablishing the old colonial solutions: dyes, mining, and cattle ranching. It was in this environment that these countries developed into nation-states after the crisis of the Federation.

Let us not be misled by the Liberal rhetoric of the reform period. Outside of secularization and a growth of power within the public sector, contrasts with the Conservative period are not all that great. The ways in which power was exercised changed little, although they did contrast notably with the noble language of the national constitutions and legislation. In practical terms, the new states are as equally heirs of the Liberal credo as they are of the Conservative restoration.

Who took power with the Liberal reforms? At least in the beginning, they were socially a heterogeneous group: landowners, merchants, middle-class urban dwellers, not to mention the many newcomers and quite a few newly converted Conservatives. What the new business establishment had in common was their vision of the opportunities for investment. Still, for the old-line businessmen, the sphere of competition was minimal, and as a result the conflict between the two establishments was almost never head on. The real losers in this new environment were certainly not the dye producers or cattle ranchers; rather they were the Indian settlements and the Church.

With the Liberal reform, the state could free up resources to develop the agricultural export economy and greatly broaden the economic basis of the new coffee producers. It might almost be said that the Liberal state "created" its own ruling class.

It is worth recapitulating now certain of the features characterizing the nation-states that were forming during the nineteenth century, although these features were not all present to the same degree or in the same way in each country:

1. Centralization of administrative, fiscal, and judicial power

2. Setting out territorial boundaries both with respect to internal control and outside recognition of sovereignty (see maps 9 and 10)

3. Creation of military and police forces to assure internal order and defense

4. A legal framework made up of constitutions, codes, and laws

5. A certain degree of bureaucratization with the concomitant lessening of personal, charismatic leadership (personalismo) and purely individual interests

6. Elements of a cultural integration, such as a nationalist ideology transmitted through public education and various forms of participation in the political system.

The last three features undoubtedly are the weakest. Bureaucracy took a long time to develop beyond purely legal structures. Personalism and arbitrariness were, in fact, the rule. Political participation was full of exclusions. This made problematical the social integration in these new nations, and this integration had to depend on older and more traditional cultural habits. The legal framework was hardly original, rather an unimaginative copy that opened the way for frequent violations of legal norms. This was, at bottom, dangerous since it set up a distance that grew ever vaster between proper conduct and actual behavior, all of which undermined an important basis for legitimacy.

In the latter half of the nineteenth century Liberal ideology underwent a significant transformation. The romantic utopian idealism of the period of independence and Federation was replaced by a pragmatic positivism that did not hesitate in using a variety of types of compromise. A good illustration is the contrast between the Nicaraguan Máximo Jerez (1818–1881) and the Guatemalan reformer Justo Rufino Barrios (1835–1885).

Máximo Jerez was a sort of Quixote: indefatigable, a dreamer obsessed with the unity of Central America. He was a lawyer, a student of the classics, and fascinated by cosmography, but he failed in almost everything he tried to do:

politics, military campaigns, and so on. In the 1860s and 1870s he became a symbol of the Morazán legacy dogged by ill-fortune just as his mentor Morazán had been. General Jerez and his Liberal friends concocted the call to Walker in 1855 and then fought brilliantly and courageously against the Filibusters but were unable to take advantage of the "National War" of 1857. Later Jerez fought in El Salvador alongside Gerardo Barrios and tried to overthrow the Nicaraguan Conservatives but was defeated in 1863. There were new ill-fated adventures in Nicaragua in 1869. With Guatemalan support in 1876, he tried once again to invade Nicaragua. This time his plan never even culminated in a single battle; the "phalanx" disintegrated as a result of disenchantment and ineptness. When Jerez died in 1881, the Honduran Adolfo Zúñiga wrote a tearful but penetrating elegy about this "sublime madman":

> A man of the old school in this calculating and Positivist century, in this century of meanness and banality, he was always a puppet and victim of the political manipulators and liars. He was too honest and sincere; he lacked that cunning spirit which assures easy but ephemeral triumphs and a false fleeting popularity.

The political realism that Jerez so sorely lacked was abundantly displayed by Justo Rufino Barrios. Barrios was energetic, authoritarian, and strong-minded. He possessed a rare sense of political opportunity. He took no half measures and put everything on the line to achieve progress. The result was a dictatorial government with an intimidated press and strong police control all legitimated by a constitution made to measure and by loyal legislators. This model would have long life in Central America just as would the periodic ritual resignation quickly retracted after tearful supplications by the Congress. Power wielded in this vein was the hallmark of efficiency in an archaic society struggling toward modernization. In this environment, the sacrifice of legal formulas and principles seemed a quite secondary concern.

The vicissitudes of the idea of a united Central America

are a good measure of the change brought about in Liberal attitudes. In the 1840s and 1850s all the Liberals were unionists. Twenty or thirty years later, things were very different. Efforts by Barrios and Zelaya were fought against by their own ideological allies. There are always some dreams that wither at the moment of their triumph.

# 4

# Impoverishing Growth (1900–1945)

Coffee exporting allowed the Central American economies to maintain an enduring relationship with world markets. This relationship entailed several very important consequences: (1) sustained economic growth, (2) strengthening of the social order initiated by the Liberal reforms, and (3) increasing subordination of the ruling class's vested interests to foreign capital and to the dynamics of foreign markets.

Expansion of coffee growing introduced fundamental structural changes in land markets, labor relations, business, and financial organization. The changes relate, on the one hand, to what was needed for coffee exports to "take off" and as such they were promoted by the Liberal reforms. On the other hand, these changes became more profound as a result of the growth itself of a coffee-based economy. In this way a single-crop economy became inevitable, introducing growing pressure on the land and labor required for subsistence agriculture.

Costa Rica's early development of coffee production served as a model for the other Central American countries. The technology of cultivation and processing of the coffee bean were mostly a result of that early experimental period and spread rapidly in the 1870s and 1880s in Guatemala and El Salvador. Having greater labor supply, the latter two countries enjoyed a clear supremacy in the Isthmus in coffee production by the end of the last century. Coffee changed and unified Central American life in the central highlands and along the Pacific Coast as no other product had. From Guatemala to Costa Rica the countryside became dotted with shady coffee fields and the harvesting, processing, and movement of the beans from November to April patterned the movement of rural workers. The methods of cultivation were similar to those employed in gardening. The plants were seeded in nursery beds and then transplanted, pruned, and weeded. Shade was provided by large trees that protected the coffee plants from the hot sun and the wind. Fertilizers and irrigation were uncommon. This is to be expected in regions with rich volcanic soils and regular rainfall. Decreasing yields were slow to appear. For this reason, the early phase of coffee growing was closely tied to the quality and intensity of the labor invested in it. It was impractical to mechanize any part of the operations in lands that were broken up and dedicated to that one permanent crop.

In Guatemala and El Salvador the agrarian landscape was dominated by a few relatively large landholdings whereas for Costa Rica the small and mid-sized coffee grower always enjoyed an important role. The labor systems also show marked contrasts. For Guatemala and El Salvador, labor conditions were particularly repressive. Sharecropping (colonato) was the usual system to guarantee a labor force. Guatemala also employed forced recruitments of Indian workers at harvest time, as well as payment by scrip and police persecution of anyone who could not prove they were employed by some landowner. In El Salvador and Costa Rica during harvests, work was paid for in cash. This similarity between the two countries should not blind us to a crucial difference: El Salvador's laborers were largely part of a landless peasantry while in Costa Rica there were small and mid-sized growers who primarily depended on family members for labor.

From the macroeconomic viewpoint, the process of accumulation in Central American coffee economies can be regarded simply as the blending of land and manual labor into the production process. Up to the 1950s, differences in yield per area, leaving aside for the moment the issue of climatic fluctuations and random influences, depended on the quality and intensity of the manual labor employed. Under these circumstances, it is obvious that economic benefits will be appropriated mainly by those who own or control the land and supply the financing for the coffee bean processing and production.

El Salvador's high population density and the massive eviction of Indians from their lands created a landless peasantry that provided an abundant and cheap source of labor. Once they possessed the land best suited for coffee growing, the producers had ideal conditions for accumulation of wealth. In Guatemala, the availability of land did not imply an abundant labor force, given the situation of the Indian settlements. To generate sufficient workers, forced labor was employed that, while not entirely optimal within a capitalist framework, did have the virtue of providing the labor necessary to increase coffee growing. For both countries, land accumulation and development of large landholdings were undoubtedly the best paths for business. In the labor markets mentioned above, wages were governed by the internal cost of reproducing the labor force. In this way the landowner–worker relation became a "zero-sum game": once land was acquired, the owners maximized their income by keeping cash labor costs to a minimum. There were no market forces in the goods-and-services marketplace that could create change in the distribution of income. Peasants could only improve their lot by becoming landowners or unionizing to collectively negotiate their wages. Let us note, however, that both options, which are typical of any reformist program, meant an especially radical transformation in the context of the socioeconomic structures in Guatemala and El Salvador.

Consider again the case of Costa Rica. Colonial evolution produced a peasantry that was free, with a strong tradition of individualism in a context of low population density and an isolated economy. The early growth of coffee production, which was labor intensive, had the virtue of reinforcing a social structure in which the small and mid-sized grower was predominant and subordinate to the merchant capital. Those who were initially the most successful in the coffee business formed a powerful ruling class whose wealth was based on a monopoly of coffee processing and the management of financial resources (credit, production financing, export). Even though these businessmen generally were also the largest landowners, their role in coffee production was secondary. The growth of the coffee economy depended on a slow and gradual colonization resulting from the settling of new families in uninhabited frontier areas. Thus the structure of small and mid-sized growers dependent on financial markets continued to reproduce itself. As time passed, however, the division of lands through inheritance and the closing of the agricultural frontier for suitable coffee-growing land (around 1930) provided a basis for creating a rural semi-proletariat.

In Costa Rica, the relationship between coffee business (financial capital and processing) and the small and mid-sized growers formed the basis for a social dynamic, although unequally. Everyone enjoyed the benefits of coffee exporting. In other terms, we can characterize this relationship as a "non–zero-sum game." Under these conditions, each sector developed typically reformist strategies; that is, each competed to improve its relative position in the market of goods and services. The institutionalization of this competition constituted a powerful factor of legitimization. The collaboration and agreement between classes was an essential feature in the slow and gradual process of creating a nation-state.

The economic boom in the region had repercussions in urbanization and imports changed to reflect the tastes and customs of the landed classes. The capital cities in Central America had been truly small villages during the nineteenth century but now took on a character much less provincial. There was even some building whose style echoed the belle epoque. The incipient middle class, tied to business and government employment, began to make a timid appearance socially.

Everything was involved in the storage and transport of the harvested coffee had major consequences for the Central American economies. Until the Panama Canal was opened,

Central American coffee (its "mild–aromatic" character was highly valued) made its way to the European consumer through a very circuitous route that included either passage along California or a maritime route around Cape Horn. The interoceanic railway through Panama was only a partial solution in that the abundant rainfall increased the costs of handling large quantities of coffee and, above all, seriously threatened its quality. The most direct solution, attempted by the governments of Costa Rica and Guatemala beginning in the 1870s, was to build railways to the Atlantic Coast and thereby utilize suitable ports there. The railway construction, when it was finally finished (Costa Rica's in 1890 and Guatemala's in 1908), produced three major changes: (1) the active penetration of foreign capital, English and U.S., (2) the starting of the banana-exporting industry, and (3) the partial opening of the Atlantic region to further colonization.

Banana-producing activities began in the 1870s with shipments from the coast of Honduras sold in New Orleans. The entrepreneur Minor Keith, who had been building the railway between Limón and San José since 1871, was experiencing serious deficits. With a branch line already operating, he decided to try to raise money shipping bananas in 1878. He was rapidly successful. Up to the close of the last century, banana exports to New Orleans were made from all along the Caribbean coastlines and were controlled by small- and medium-sized companies who owned the vessels while the production was undertaken by local growers. Land concessions around the railway lines, however, widened the commercial possibilities to an unexpected degree. Now one could have plantations in the interior of the country and increase the scale of production. The control of docks and piers and the use of larger vessels with refrigerated holds completed the requirements for dealing with a perishable product whose transit time was carefully calculated. The United Fruit Company, formed in 1899 with $11 million in U.S. capital, combined land concessions to U.S. businessmen centered in Costa Rica and Colombia. Together with the Cuyamel Fruit Company set up by Samuel Zemurray merged with United Fruit in 1929–and the Standard Fruit and Steamship Company, the three monopolized the banana trade throughout the entire Caribbean and Central America region.

The Atlantic coastal regions of Central America from Guatemala to Panama took on a new aspect. Salaried laborers brought in from Jamaica worked the large U.S.-owned plantations. These Afro-American immigrants mixed with the few inhabitants of the same origin who had lived in these regions since the seventeenth century and strengthened their Caribbean cultural traits, thereby separating even further this "other" Central America from that of the central highlands and the Pacific Coast. The banana companies' relative sovereignty no doubt reinforced them as microcosms. With their own transportation systems, schools, hospitals, communication systems, and commissaries, these were truly separate enclaves in the tropical forests.

The foreign capital, particularly U.S. capital, entering the region after World War, tied the Isthmus ever-more tightly to world markets. Even though coffee production continued to reside in the hands of local growers, it was increasingly foreign ownership that dominated output. Although the German growers in Guatemala, to take an example, controlled only 10 percent of the coffee plantations in 1913, they produced 40 percent of the total harvest. The powerful banana companies whose interests extended widely into plantations, railways, shipping lines, vessels, communications companies, and so forth, had an increasingly important role. Functioning as spokesmen for the Central American governments, they tended to represent internationally the imperialist interests of foreign investment.

Forty or fifty years later the fruits of this agroexport development were still meager. The Central American countries were small producers within the overall world economy and were very susceptible to economic fluctuations elsewhere. Their economies had barely seen any diversification and their principal exports, coffee and bananas, were only "desserts" for European or U.S. consumers. The high qual-

ity of Central American coffee was not enough to compensate for the disadvantages of a single-crop economy. And
banana plants were extremely vulnerable to pests and disease, sometimes leading to whole regions being abandoned,
heightening unemployment and rural poverty.

The internal integration of the national economies was
slow and unequal. The agroexport sector only slightly impacted economic diversification. Put differently, production
for export created very few additional economic activities in
the primary and secondary sectors. Only business and services enjoyed a significant expansion and that was natural
up to a point for small national economies with relatively
small populations and limited consumer markets. Internal
consumer demand basically was satisfied with imported
goods and those produced for self-consumption in agricultural production. If one examines the makeup of imports
according to product type, it is symptomatic that between
the end of the nineteenth century and the 1950s there were
few changes to be seen: around 50 percent of imports were
of nondurable goods.

The colonization of unpopulated areas depended on their
having uncultivated land available, on transportation facilities, and on national policies guaranteeing opportunity for
ownership of land. Albeit slowly and unevenly, agrarian capitalism invaded these areas. But what happened in the
newly colonized areas was entirely driven by the dynamics
of an agroexport economy. This implied, therefore, very few
changes in the character of the social structure.

To summarize, development in the agroexport sector did
not push toward a deep expansion of capitalism by adding
new productive sectors, incorporating new technologies,
and increasing labor productivity. In other words, the
agroexport sector did not act as a growth multiplier. The sum
total of economic activity always remained in the thrall of
the vicissitudes of the international marketplace.

Foreign economic crises, such as those of coffee prices
between 1897 and 1908, World War I, or the stock market
collapse of 1929, could only have the overall effect of re-

tarding these rather undiversified economies. For the large landowners, those circumstances had clear advantages since they allowed large landowners to maintain their system and preserve the coffee plantations while awaiting better times.

## EL SEÑOR PRESIDENTE: THE THEORY AND PRACTICE OF LIBERAL POLITICS

It was not the existence of societies with deep inequalities that characterized Central America's uniqueness; rather, it was in how these imbalances were translated politically into an exclusion of the underclasses. In practice, the life of Liberal institutions and laws was above all an immense "monologue" of the ruling classes with themselves.

Coup d'etats, controlled elections, and candidates imposed by the government were the norm in presidential successions. Legislative assemblies struggled in the context of their limited authority vis-à-vis a dominant executive and difficulties in working as a collegiate body. Frequently debates ended up in hurling insults or violent scuffles. A seat in an assembly represented barely a minor reward of employment patronage with the meager political pie.

Public opinion did not exist. There were, certainly, public demonstrations, emotions, secret rumors or hinted criticisms buried "between the lines" of a press that was almost always censored. In a spirit of bitter resignation the Nicaraguan Enrique Guzmán Selva wrote the following in his personal diary concerning the 1902 Honduran elections:

> October 27: Beginning last Sunday that old, tiresome and grotesque farce Central Americans call "presidential elections" is taking place. We have all known the outcome for some time. I am fascinated to see how serious people still can participate in such a comedy.

Given differing degrees of violence and certain purely local touches, this description is valid wherever we travel in Central America and whether we go forward or backward in time.

In actuality, a separation of powers did not exist. "Extraordinary authority" and "state of emergency" were broadly used legal artifices that allowed some camouflage of the executive branch's enduring preeminence and frequent abuse of power. Under "extraordinary authority" the president legislated at his own discretion during congressional recesses. With a "state of emergency" individual rights and civil liberties were suspended under the slightest internal or external pretext. This invariably meant persecution and control of the political opposition.

The concentration of power in few hands and the political weakness of the landed classes' organizations created an ample arena for charismatic leadership (personalismo) by dictators as typical as Manuel Estrada Cabrera, the "Señor Presidente" of Miguel Angel Asturias's marvelous novel.

A strong paternalism, not without a mythic halo, assured personal loyalty expressed through blind obedience and continual adulation. The network of henchmen ended up in any case as a secret police producing a chain of accusations that was particularly effective. Successive reelections, each preceded by a "resignation" repealed after outbursts of sincerity that were as vehement as they were suspicious, were another typical ingredient requiring adroit juggling of much-abused constitutions.

These dictators never ceased to represent the overall interest of the agroexport oligarchy. Yet in their absolute power they generated inner contradictions and conflicts, and another potentially dangerous element: with the years, the dictator's power became spent and he fell from office through civil war or a collective outburst of fury. To have had, rather, a republic of distinguished citizens with its leadership recruited from the leading families, along with a rotation of the offices, would have been a much more rational arrangement. In reality, this was the situation in El Salvador between 1898 and 1931, and it also characterized Nicaragua during the nineteenth century under the "Thirty Years" Conservative rule. In both countries the formulas were unstable due to the obvious inability of the ruling classes to undertake a change in the political system. In Nicaragua, Granadan families formed the heart of the Conservative elite. They proved incapable of broadening their social base and fell before the pressures of the Liberal businessmen of Managua and León under the leadership of José Santos Zelaya. In El Salvador, the ruling class opened up the political system too late (in 1931) to contain the social unrest that led with blistering rapidity to a revolution and bloody massacre. Afterward, political power was permanently delegated to the military.

In conclusion, personal dictatorship seems to have been a sort of recurring necessity of the oligarchic system. There are two reasons that may make this understandable. The first arises from the fact that the agroexport oligarchies developed and became a class, socioeconomically speaking, at the same time they took political power. This fact allowed plenty of room for friction and internecine struggles between factions and active roles for newcomers. The second has to do with the enormous amount of violence and repression that lay at the very heart of an agroexport economy itself. Without a strong government, economic growth became doubtful.

In Guatemala this panorama lasted without interruption from Barrios up through the fall of Ubico in 1944 and including those long twenty-two years of Manuel Estrada Cabrera's dictatorship from 1898 to 1920. The strategies of governing in Guatemala can be briefly summarized as: censorship of the press, exile and prison for the opposition, extensive police control, a reduced and servile state bureaucracy, matters of finance and the treasury in the hands of interrelated members of the large coffee-growing families, and benevolent treatment of foreign companies.

The "Minerva Festivals" (Fiestas de Minerva) held under the wing of Guatemala's "Teacher and Protector of Youth" inspired praise in the Central American press and fulfilled an important legitimizing role. Guatemala City was transformed into a novel "tropical Athens." The intellectuals were not stingy in their praise: Gómez Carrillo, from Paris, José Santos Chocano, and Rubén Darío himself. Darío wrote:

> Here appears again, austere,
> the great and luminous Minerva;
> the Goddess's right hand arose
> and governing wingless Minerva's gesture
> was the land of Estrada Cabrera.

They called him a "new Pericles," the "great priest of the wise Minerva," and many other heroic titles. No one seemed the slightest concerned that public education was a disgrace, that the budget of the Ministry of Navy and War was eight or ten times greater than that of Public Instruction.

The fall of Estrada Cabrera in 1920 was led by the Central American Unionist Party (El Partido Unionista Centroamericano). This alliance of intellectuals, students, and the middle classes, however, was quickly displaced from power. In 1921 General Orellana, who had been a lieutenant of the former dictator, took control of the presidency.

There was, in any case, some loosening of the oligarchy's power especially during the rule of General Lázaro Chacón, who took over from Orellana in 1926. The economic prosperity of Guatemala during this period allowed some institutional modernization and stabilized the currency. Particularly important was the creation of the National Labor Department (Departamento Nacional del Trabajo) and passage of several pieces of legislation that protected workers' rights, in reaction to an upsurge of unionism and worker associations. Social unrest was also reflected by several new political groups that formed, such as the Cooperativist Party (Partido Cooperativista), the Labor Party (Partido Laborista,) and the Guatemalan Communist Party (Partido Comunista de Guatemala). The University of San Carlos was granted autonomy, and after 1921 the Men's Teachers' College School (Escuela Normal de Varones) became a hotbed of critical thought and new ideas. This new atmosphere suffered a drastic break in 1930 when General Chacón suddenly died.

His passing raised the issue of presidential succession amidst the world economic crisis, and General Orellana headed up a military coup in December of that year. Lack of U.S. diplomatic recognition, however, consistent with the 1923 Washington Accords, made it necessary to call for elections in February of 1931. General Jorge Ubico, who won the presidency, had an enviable background. He had been the chief of staff, civil chief (*jefe político*) in Retalhuleu and Alta Verapaz, congressman on several occasions, and secretary of defense under General Orellana. He ruled with an iron hand until 1944.

In a way, Ubico repeated the system of Estrada Cabrera, but with a more modern and efficient style. He reorganized the secret police and terrorized the opposition. Between 1931 and 1934, workers' organizations were decimated, the University of San Carlos lost its autonomy, and dissidents were silenced. The government strongly promoted agriculture, generous concessions to foreign investors, financial stability, and an ambitious public works effort. Construction of roads and buildings was vigorously pursued and occasionally even witnessed Ubico's personal leadership in projects.

Forced labor recruiting was rejuvenated now under provisions of the Public Roadways Law (Ley de Vialidad) requiring two weeks a year of obligatory public service, which also could be satisfied by a specified payment. Also enacted were harsh decrees against vagrancy. Debt peonage, typically faced by rural laborers, was suppressed in 1935, at which time the civil chiefs acquired greater control over labor and displaced the landowners' control. Centralization of state power was completed when the system of intendants appointed directly by the president replaced the local mayors (Alcaldes). In this fashion the local "bosses" became less important and the "chief executive" was able to exercise great control over the various interest groups.

In 1941 the Ubico regime reached its zenith. Obedient legislators petitioned the president to continue in office until 1949. World War II, however, contributed to tarnishing the image of administrative order and efficiency. Ubico did not hide his affinity for Spain's Franco. Even though he had obediently heeded all the U.S. demands regarding the war effort and had kept a prudent distance from the Axis, the international press did not hesitate to label him a fascist. By the end of the war he had become a very discomfiting voice.

In El Salvador the combination of authoritarianism and paternalism that was a direct descendant of the Liberal period of the 1870s dominated absolutely between 1898 and 1931. In fact, members of a single family, the Meléndez-Quiñónez family, rotated the presidency among themselves between 1913 and 1927. This pattern suffered a crisis during the Great Depression of 1930. A growing labor movement in the cities reached as well into the coffee-growing areas, and social unrest was uninterrupted at the close of the 1920s. The disarray of the ruling class and the prosperity that the country had experienced before the Great Depression allowed the government of Pío Romero Bosque (1927–1931), enlightened Conservative, to legalize unions and put forth some labor laws. Even though at the close of his regime he ordered some persecution, he did permit free elections for his successor and guaranteed freedom of the press. The January 1931 elections established Arturo Araujo as president. He was a good-hearted landowner educated in London, and he sincerely admired the English labor movement. His election was brought about through support from a variety of union and intellectual groups. Among these the figure of Alberto Masferrer stands out. Araujo scarcely ruled for ten months during which time the painful pent-up effects of the economic crisis fell upon the workers. The landowners were horrified at Araujo's vaguely socialist ideas. Inefficiency in the administration along with serious fiscal problems, which included inability to pay civil servants and the military, precipitated the crisis. On the second of December, 1931, a coup d'etat erupted in which General Maximiliano Hernández Martínez, who had been vice-president and minister of war under Araujo, took over the government. By January 1932 a general insurrection seized El Salvador: Indians and mestizos armed with machetes and sticks rose up all throughout the coffee-producing region while the government arrested and shot the leaders of the newly founded (1925) El Salvador Communist Party that was led by Farabundo Martí. A repression followed upon the uprising and ended with somewhere between 10,000 and 30,000 dead. This insurrection and the repression that followed it have deeply marked contemporary Salvadorean history. The landowners gave up trying to rule the country and delegated that authority to the military, but they contributed to organizing a particularly repressive system. The peasants entered into the shadow of forty years of oppressed silence.

Hernández Martínez shared Ubico's virtues and style along with a similar political and economic program. Public works and moderate state intervention, such as the Debt Relief Law (Ley de Moratoria) postponing all loans due payments, setting up the Central Bank and so forth, were blended into a clear corporate mentality favoring institutional changes benefiting the propertied class.

In Honduras and Nicaragua the power structures followed along similar lines. Spawned of incomplete Liberal revolutions, they suffered heightened fragmentation due to regional vested interests. In the case of Honduras these were represented in the actions of the banana companies, while for Nicaragua there was the U.S. occupation of the country between 1912 and 1933.

Honduran politics was profoundly unstable between the 1890s and 1933. Honduras was the easy pawn of neighbors: Estrada Cabrera in Guatemala and Zelaya in Nicaragua. The weakness of its administration reveals at bottom the lack of an export economy and also of a true ruling class. The banana companies filled the first void and aggravated the second. Conflicts between the companies, their competition for land concessions, and control of the small but strategically vital Honduran National Railways all complicated an already intricate network of political intrigue. Real stability was attained under a strongman cut from the cloth of Estrada Cabrera and Ubico: Tiburcio Carías Andino. This "Doctor and General" ruled Hondurans with an iron hand but favored the banana companies with a velvet glove from 1932 to 1948.

It may be that the essential secret of Carías's stable authoritarian and paternalistic rule lay in the United Fruit and Cuyamel Fruit companies merger in 1929 which ended the struggles between them.

Nicaragua's long history is also replete with turbulent political struggles whose international aspects are also more evident. The United States intervened in 1912 to combat "a barbaric and corrupt regime." It acquired from docile and Conservative strongmen, who were anointed into office through fraudulent "democratic" elections, the Bryan–Chamorro Treaty of 1916. By this treaty the United States received (1) the right in perpetuity to construct a canal crossing Nicaragua, (2) a ninety-nine year concession of the Corn Islands (Islas del Maiz) in the Caribbean, and (3) the right to establish a naval base in the Gulf of Fonseca. This guaranteed the defense of the Panama Canal. The United States converted Nicaragua into a virtual protectorate: it controlled the customs collections, the railways, and the National Bank, all while the U.S. Marines assured internal peace. This rebuilding of Nicaragua, however, was ephemeral. Once the Marines had left in 1925, a civil war broke out again with the Liberals receiving weapons from the Mexican government. The Marines returned in 1926 and this time had to face a truly popular guerrilla struggle. An agreement was ratified in Tipitapa in March of 1927. General Moncada who was the leader of the Liberals gave up his rebellion and took over the presidency in 1928.

César Augusto Sandino roundly rejected negotiating with the U.S. occupation forces and decided to continue fighting. His forces were unexpectedly successful from their bases in the Nueva Segovia region and kept the invaders in check for several years. His nationalist, anti-imperialist banner was popular beyond the borders of Nicaragua. It enjoyed support throughout Central America and even modest support from the Mexican government.

Moncada endeavored to end the stay of the U.S. officials in Nicaragua. To that end, the National Guard was trained by U.S. instructors to replace the Marines. In 1932 the U.S.

agreed to withdraw its forces. An agreement was reached with the Sandinista rebels who turned in their weapons and, by January of 1934, everything seemed ready to create a lasting peace. That next month, however, Sandino and his lieutenants were treacherously murdered by the National Guard, who by now had its own strongman: Anastasio Somoza García.

Somoza shared many of the "virtues" of Carías Andino: an iron hand and a certain paternalism. But his power base in the National Guard was soon increased with his involvement in a diversity of businesses. He was an unswerving ally of the United States and ruled Nicaragua until he was assassinated in 1956.

Costa Rica's situation could not be more surprising given its Central American neighbors. There were regular elections with direct voting from 1912 and only one break in constitutional rule. This was the take-over in 1917 that installed Federico Tinoco. His regime barely lasted two years, and in 1919 constitutional rule was restored. The labor movement developed with relative freedom under the influence of both the social Christian and socialist ideologies. The Reformist Party (Partido Reformista) under the leadership of Jorge Volio was especially influential during the 1920s whereas during the 1930s unrest among the banana workers (there was a strike in 1934) revealed propitious conditions for the developing communist movement. The Costa Rican Communist Party was founded in 1931 by Manuel Mora Valverde.

These social tensions appear within the framework of a nation under the sway of a pragmatic liberalism influenced by reformist tendencies. President Ricardo Jiménez, for example, nationalized the insurance industry in 1924, incorporating it into the government, and did not hesitate to intervene in a limited way on a national level during the crisis of the 1930s (Banking Reform of 1936). In 1942 President Calderón Guardia adopted social legislation that synthesized the demands of the labor movement, the Communist Party, and the Catholic Church. This latter coincidence of interests illustrates better than any other example the Costa Rican

"gradualism" in the context of a Central America full of remarkable contrasts.

## SOCIAL CHANGE

The development in the Isthmus of agricultural exporting
economies entailed certain features in the social structures
that emerged. These are, briefly: (1) an enormous concentration and predominance of power in the hands of landowners, (2) a tendency to expropriate land from the Indian
peasants thereby imposing a distribution of the nation's
lands that the peasants never accepted as legitimate, (3) a
high degree of violence required for the functioning of the
new economic and political structures, and (4) a strong class
polarization along with structural weakness in the emerging
middle sectors.

These economies diversified very slowly. This fact had
repercussions throughout a frozen social structure having
barely any drive toward transformation. In other words,
there were few opportunities for social mobility in a situation
of overall backwardness and poverty.

Without retracting the overall picture presented above,
some institutional changes began to complicate social co-
hesiveness. The professionalization of the military was one
such change. The first officer-training academy was set up
in El Salvador in 1868, but the Escuela Politécnica de Guatemala established in 1873 soon became a well-known model.
This professionalization remained limited to the officer
corps. Ordinary soldiers were recruited from among the
peasants and normally were badly paid. If they were lucky
at the end of their term of service they might have learned
how to read and write. Alongside the regular army, the police agencies also began to professionalize themselves and
rigorously train for repression. The El Salvadorean National
Guard, organized in 1912 and modeled after the Spanish
Civil Guard, and the Nicaraguan National Guard, which itself was directly born of U.S. occupation, are the best-known
examples.

In Honduras and Costa Rica the way the military developed took different paths. For Honduras, professionalization occurred much later: it began in 1950. For Costa Rica, it never took place. After Tinoco fell from power in 1919, the Costa Rican Army was discredited and deteriorated. This loss of status finally culminated in 1949 when the Armed Forces were constitutionally abolished.

Even though the main social role of armies and police forces has always been one of repression, we should not lose sight of their function as a vehicle for social mobility, at least for the officer corps. This issue becomes more significant precisely in the context of extremely polarized social structures where the emerging middle sectors are small.

Education played a secondary role. Ambitious plans for universal education, typical of the Liberal epoch, existed only on paper except in the case of Costa Rica. The vast majority of the rural population remained illiterate. In government budgets, the amounts budgeted for "public instruction" were always low and invariably two or three times smaller than the military budgets. Universities had a mediocre existence and were limited to the training of lawyers and a few other professional careers. As a result, nonetheless, of the Córdoba Reform in 1918 and the Mexican Revolution, they became seed beds of new ideas and sometimes sources of opposition to the oligarchy.

Labor unions appeared slowly and in a hostile, repressive environment. The first ones unionized shoemakers, carpenters, bakers, and so forth; in short, various craft workers in the urban areas. They began, however, to show increased activity after World War I. Unionization was common to all five Central American nations but it was especially important in El Salvador. The Regional Workers Federation of El Salvador (Federación Regional de Trabajadores de El Salvador) was formed in 1924 and held annual congresses until 1931. Parallel to this, there were Central American delegates to the Latin American Labor Congress held in Montevideo in 1929 and strong connections with the International Red Aid (Socorro Rojo Internacional) headquartered in New York. Participation by Mexican activists was noticed with some misgivings by U.S. diplomats who regarded it as part of a plan orchestrated by the Third International. Strikes and labor conflicts were commonplace in the banana-growing regions and likewise for the mines in Nicaragua and Honduras. This first phase in the growth of the Central American labor movement culminated with two outstanding events on the eve of the 1930 Depression. One was the creation of Communist parties that belonged to the Third International. The other shortly thereafter was a way of repression that, in Guatemala, Honduras, El Salvador, and Nicaragua, eliminated most of those organizations or confined them to an illegality that prohibited significant activities.

"Political parties" at this time characteristically were groups that congregated around certain leaders and which scarcely had platforms. A typical example of this can be found in the "differences" between the Liberals and Conservatives in Nicaragua and Honduras. These two parties were apparently more stable than those alliances formed for sham elections which were the norm for El Salvador and Guatemala. Even in Costa Rica there were no active parties having a well-defined ideological base until the 1940s. Despite many limitations, politics constituted another channel for social mobility. Selective advancements by means of favoritism, theft, undercutting political enemies, or other stratagems were commonplace among the hangers-on around such dictators as Ubico, Carías, Estrada Cabrera, or Somoza.

Intellectual utopias and programs of action sometimes combined with sincere efforts to understand and change Central American social reality. The Nicaraguan Salvador Mendieta (1882–1958) led the Central American Unionist Party (Partido Unionista Centroamericano) organized by Guatemalan students in 1899. He had a blind faith in a Central American Union and attributed most of the Isthmus's misfortunes to separatism. His major work, *The Sickness of Central America* (*La enfermedad de Centro-América*), was completed during the 1930s and published in three volumes. Its style and method derive from nineteenth century positivism: first a "description of the subject and symptoms of the disease," second a "diagnosis of the disease," and third a "cure." Unionism is the basic principle of the cure, along with a certain moral code.

More original and further removed from Liberal canons is the thought of Alberto Masferrer (1868–1932). His doctrine of a "Vital Minimum" set forth a "limit to be respected by those who control and hoard wealth" and minimal necessities that a worker must have fulfilled (housing, justice, adequate wages, and so forth). With mutual renunciation and love of one's neighbor those values could be practiced and thereby give rise to a new philosophy or religion. The state itself should concern itself with enforcing those values.

Anti-imperialism and the recovery of national autonomy are the essential features of Sandino's (1895–1934) and Vicente Sáenz's (1896–1963) thinking. Sandino's ideas developed in the course of his guerrilla struggles in Nicaragua from 1926 to 1934. Sáenz evolved his ideas in the context of long years in journalism and education which began in Costa Rica in the 1920s and continued in Mexico after 1941. Both writers share the same Latin American spirit, the same unionist fervor, and a similar strong concern for the welfare of the numerous peasants and workers suffering from backwardness, low status, and oppression. They also kept their distance from the Third International; Vicente Sáenz eventually declared himself to be a socialist reformer.

Let us now return to a more global perspective while still proceeding country by country.

In Guatemala, intense class polarization was compensated by the relative absence of expropriation of Indian communal lands in the high plains. But this same circumstance inevitably led to the Indians' forced labor and also to solidifying prejudice toward them founded on the notion of their "racial" inferiority. The end result was to create a culturally divided society that had become frozen in the milieu of a lost past.

El Salvador had seen from the beginning an even greater and more unmitigated class polarization. Its origins lie in the complete expropriation of communal Indian and ladino lands, in the denser, more concentrated population, and in a more advanced acculturation process stemming from the colonial period. When the 1932 rebellion was repressed, that event completed the cultural unification of the Salvadorean peasantry. Perhaps as a result, the reaction to an imposed order by the landowning classes was quicker, more coordinated, and more violent in El Salvador than in any of the neighboring countries. U.S. diplomats were careful observers of the 1932 insurrection and soon discovered the "conditions that allowed the rapid rise of so-called communism." The observers reported, not without some apprehension, that "the rural laborers were miserably paid and on many ranches put up with intolerable conditions." Indeed, they also observed that "it is often said that for a landowner, a farm animal is worth much more than a laborer, since there is such an abundance of hands."

Honduras is replete with violent contrasts. On the banana plantations and in the mines a typical proletariat developed: a salaried population more or less continuously employed throughout the year. By the end of the 1920s, there were some 22,000 banana workers of whom some 80 percent labored on the plantations themselves with the remainder working on the docks or the railway. Compared with this, the miners were numerically insignificant. During this same period the San Jacinto Mine, run by the Rosario Mining Company, recorded slightly over 1,000 workers, a number hardly changed from the beginning of the century. Unionization struggles began early on in both areas and enjoyed remarkable success in the 1920s. Even though unionization was repressed drastically during the Carías dictatorship, it formed a basis for union development that by the end of the 1950s was already appearing to be the most advanced in

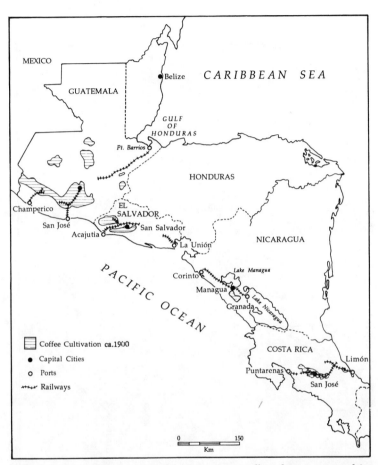

**Map 11.** The coffee-growing regions are small and concentrated in the volcanically rich soil of the highlands. This facilitated creating a rail link with the Pacific and Atlantic coast ports. The railway network would be completed years later: in 1908 Guatemala and Port Barrios were linked; in 1929 branch lines connecting with the El Salvador railway were completed.

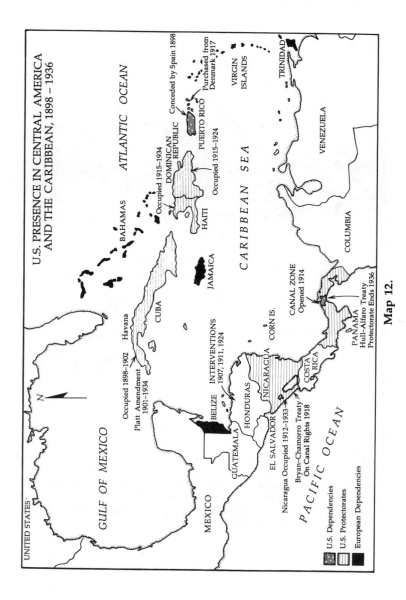

U.S. PRESENCE IN CENTRAL AMERICA
AND THE CARIBBEAN, 1898 – 1936

UNITED STATES

N

GULF OF MEXICO

MEXICO

GUATEMALA

BELIZE

HONDURAS

EL SALVADOR

NICARAGUA

COSTA
RICA

PANAMA

PACIFIC OCEAN

ATLANTIC OCEAN

BAHAMAS

CUBA

Havana

Occupied 1898–1902
Platt Amendment
1901–1934

INTERVENTIONS
1907, 1911, 1924

CORN IS.

CANAL ZONE
Opened 1914

Hull–Alfaro Treaty
Protectorate Ends 1936

Nicaragua Occupied 1912–1933

Bryan–Chamorro Treaty 1912
On Canal Rights 1918

JAMAICA

CARIBBEAN SEA

COLUMBIA

VENEZUELA

DOMINICAN
REPUBLIC

Occupied 1915–1934

HAITI

Occupied 1915–1924

PUERTO RICO

Conceded by Spain 1898

Purchased from
Denmark 1917

VIRGIN
ISLANDS

TRINIDAD

U.S. Dependencies

U.S. Protectorates

European Dependencies

Map 12.

Central America. Although it was strong and organized on the plantations, the agricultural proletariat was a minority in the overall fragmented economy of Honduras. Those 22,000 workers represented perhaps 10 percent of the total male labor force. The other 90 percent primarily consisted of the most backward and isolated peasantry in all Central America.

In Nicaragua there may have been fewer varieties of contrast but the peasantry itself was equally divided. The cattle ranches competed with coffee plantations, while in the Nueva Segovia region there was some minimal mining development. Under these diverse conditions, afflicted by civil wars, there ruled a paternalism that was much more traditional. It changed only in recent times partly due to the rise of the Somoza family and the rapid expansion of cotton exports in the 1950s.

Costa Rica is a true enigma. What are the social foundations that would account for its continual representative democracy and early successful reforms? Coffee growing brought together small and middle-sized landholdings with some large plantations whose owners controlled processing and sales. Low population density, combined with a crop requiring intensive labor per acre, was a structural factor that prevented the complete concentration of lands into large plantations but promoted a rapid proletarization. As we remarked before, early reforms were made possible by a less-polarized society and by an economically weaker ruling class than was to be found among their peers in Guatemala or El Salvador. The middle sectors involved in production of export crops unquestionably provided a social base allowing representative democracy to function as well as broadening the mechanisms for political participation.

## BIG NEIGHBOR, GOOD STICK

Strategic interests, and in particular defense of the Panama Canal, have been a permanent leitmotif in U.S. policy toward Central America and the Caribbean. Indeed, the continually increasing U.S. global responsibilities throughout the twentieth century have been parallel to a growing obsession over the security of the region. Around this nucleus of fundamental interests have been woven various ideological webs to justify policies and conduct. One can perceive some surprisingly continuous threads that extend through the terms of American presidents from John Kennedy to Ronald Reagan. Earlier on, Theodore Roosevelt did not hesitate to appeal, whenever "chronic examples" presented themselves or some governments were demonstrably incapable of behaving properly in the international arena, to what has come to be known as the "Roosevelt Corollary" (1904) of the Monroe Doctrine. The Monroe Doctrine supposed that the United States had a "civilizing mission" in the Western Hemisphere. In these instances, the Monroe Doctrine of 1823, aptly summarized in the famous phrase "America for the Americans," justified the United States to act in the role of an "international police force." Woodrow Wilson, between 1913 and 1921, changed the emphasis away from such inflamed moralism, softening the face but not the body of that "civilizing mission." Franklin D. Roosevelt's "Good Neighbor" policy (1933–1945) was likewise not far from those roots. The essence boils down in the end to sharing with these countries the marvels of the "American Success," to extending to them the virtues of progress by peaceful means.

It is therefore understandable that few breaks are evident in U.S. policy toward Latin America and, in particular, toward Central America and the Caribbean. The definition of "new" policies was prompted either by the emergence of new interests, both economic and political, that were complementary to the main threads already cited or by a change in the U.S. State Department's perceptions. But these new policies never came to mean a complete reversal from the means and methods followed before. Thus, it is better to talk about "new styles" that sought to enrich the rather unvarying relations between the United States and its closest neighbors south of the Rio Grande. That everpresent blend of contempt, pity, and superiority has always been an ideological trait too strong for any other intentions to emerge.

Direct military interventions, strategic territorial concessions, and protectorates all formed the policy of the Big Stick established by Theodore Roosevelt (1901–1909). The 1901 Platt Amendment imposed upon the new Cuban Republic conceded to the United States, among other benefits, the right to intervene in that nation's affairs. Panama owed its independence in 1903 to the support of the U.S. fleet, and two weeks after independence the Canal Treaty was signed (November 18, 1903) conceding to the United States territorial rights in the zone where the canal was to be built. A year earlier England and Germany had blockaded the Venezuelan coast in a gesture apparently foreshadowing a major intervention. Their motives were repayment of a sizeable debt by a Venezuela weakened from civil wars and corruption. Teddy Roosevelt mediated, and in February 1903 a compromise was reached that ended the blockade. This lesson served to prevent a similar incident with the Dominican Republic where in 1905 the customs collections began to be administered by U.S. officials under the protection of several nearby warships. Financial and economic relationships throughout the whole Caribbean area had been reshaped. The weight of U.S. interests grew rapidly. British involvement increasingly stagnated. London allowed Washington to join in inciting a stubborn blockade against Germany's attempts to penetrate the region. When the Panama Canal was inaugurated in 1914, it became the centerpiece of this new arrangement and legitimized the U.S. presence in the whole political and economic life of the area.

The Treaties of 1907 tried to put an end to the frequent conflicts between Central American nations under the guarantee of Mexico and the United States. A Central American Court of Justice was established to arbitrate the conflicts and the Tovar Doctrine of not recognizing governments that came to power unconstitutionally was adopted. Honduras's neutrality was agreed to as well since this was Central Amer-

ica's weakest nation and thus one suffering continual interference by neighbors. Revolutionary activity by political
groups was outlawed in all the region's countries. This piece
of diplomacy, the product of the mutual interests of Teddy
Roosevelt and Porfirio Díaz, soon fell apart. Nothing could
be more utopian than the attempt to guarantee the status
quo in turbulent and volatile Central America. It was soon
revealed that not even the principal guarantor, the United
States felt disposed to seriously fulfill the Treaties' principles, not to mention the unwilling signatory countries. The
fall of Zelaya in 1909 occasioned the first example of non-
compliance.

President Taft (1909–1913) introduced a significant new
variant. Diplomatic activity and military intervention would
back up the development of investments and actions by U.S.
businesses. In this way Dollar Diplomacy was shaped as the
effective counterpart of the Big Stick in a period of rapidly
expanding U.S. investments in banana plantations, mining,
and railways. The most revealing index to this new situation
could be found in how foreign debts were handled. It was
only a few short years before New York bankers replaced
European bondholders and became the principal creditors of
Central American governments. Control of customs revenues, a secure income source, and military intervention to
protect U.S. property and citizens, became the policies most
often invoked.

None of this prevented political turmoil. The Isthmus experienced an almost endemic instability. Yet from the viewpoint of U.S. interests, there was undeniable success. The
military bases held under long-term lease and the Bryan–
Chamorro Treaty adequately guaranteed the security of the
Canal, while U.S. companies acquired preferences and mag-
nanimous concessions.

The Washington Accords ratified in 1923 by the five Central American republics and the United States essentially rei-
terated the provisions of the 1907 Treaty. The pacts' practical
effects were, however, rather limited. If during the 1920s
there was a lessening of regional conflicts, that could be at-

tributed to an increased consolidation of the nation states and especially to the continual U.S. military presence in Nicaragua.

Franklin D. Roosevelt's Good Neighbor policy was, on the surface, a very drastic change. It ended the protectorates and abrogated the rights to intervene in Cuba and Panama. This seemed to inaugurate a true "New Deal" for the U.S.-dominated Isthmus. The political stability of the region and cessation of interventions were, however, the outcome of an unmistakable equation involving dictators. Somoza, Ubico, Hernández Martínez, and Carías were, like Trujillo and Batista, better guarantors of a *Pax Americana* than the U.S. Marines themselves.

The economic crisis of the 1930s and World War II compelled greater cooperation. Bilateral trade treaties, agreements on strategic products, privileged entry into U.S. markets, and increasing cooperation between the government in Washington and its Central American counterparts became evident. The coffee accords signed in 1940, in which all Latin American producers participated, constituted perhaps the best example of the new situation. The quota system guaranteed the Central American countries sale of their principal export at the critical moment when the door to European markets was closing.

No one can doubt Franklin D. Roosevelt's sincerity in his stance toward Latin America: nonintervention, noninterference, and reciprocity were clearly present in U.S.–Latin American relations during the 1930s and World War II. Even when some countries impinged on U.S. economic interests by nationalist actions, the U.S. reaction was moderate and remained within diplomatic channels. Yet the Good Neighbor policy also rested on the expectation that Latin American governments and military would cooperate with the United States with little hesitation. World War II was the first test of the policy and the results were undeniably successful. The Cold War was the second. Now, however, old problems resurfaced. Guatemala in 1954 and the Dominican Republic in 1965, to pick only two examples, witnessed a revival of

Teddy Roosevelt's Big Stick. Thus were demonstrated not only the continuity of that policy but the depth of the sincerity that lay behind the rhetoric.

# 5

# Growing Inequalities (1945–1980)

## REFORM MOVEMENTS IN PERSPECTIVE

At the close of the World War II a new epoch seemed to open. The fall of Ubico and Hernández Martínez in 1944 was the first sign of these new times. Coffee prices rose greatly and remained high throughout the whole decade of the 1950s assuring a comfortable level of prosperity after the war.

Underdevelopment and social problems acquired new relevance. Under the aura of the United Nations charter and of various other missions and bodies, well-known problems began to be diagnosed and a wide range of solutions proposed. These concerns found their social roots in the worries of the middle classes and often ended up helping satisfy genuine needs of the working and peasant classes. Various reform programs were supported concurrently by professors, university students, public officials, some professional groups, owners of small businesses, urban crafts workers, and some military officers. The overall thrust of the reforms can be easily stated. Socially, there was the struggle for social security, the workers' rights to organize, and adoption of labor laws. Economically, the recovery included some state control of the banks and credit, plans for agrarian reform or change, and a policy of diversification. Politically, there were pressures to respect the constitution and suffrage and to make representative democracy work. There were also some nationalist efforts to recover control, such as fiscal control of the banana companies, to complete the character of these programs.

Success or failure of reform efforts depended fundamentally on three factors. First, there was the capacity of the ruling classes to react. They tended to view any concession as the first link in a chain that would end up in social revolution. In the propitious Cold War environment, they took recourse behind anticommunist ideology to close their ranks and label as communist even the most timorous of reforms. Second, there was the importance of the middle classes, their means of political expression, and their ability to command broad-based support. Third, particularly in the international context, there was a readiness of the United States in its foreign policy to sacrifice any declaration of good intentions in the service of strategic interests.

What was most significant in the wave of reforms is the crucial distinction between reforms as such and their actual impact. The ruling classes ended up accepting after a period of struggle and conflict a combination of changes that they saw as a sign of the times. However, this only meant the changes were formally adopted rather than translated into real alterations in class relations. This is what happened with labor laws, which frequently were not enforced, or the administration of social security, or the manipulation of bank credit in favor of the privileged. In any case, the formal existence of laws and institutions that answered in a major way the real needs and desires of the masses was important as a banner in the struggle of unions and political parties. It contributed favorably towards political mobilization and collective political awareness. In other words, a new space had opened up for the dispossessed where they could more openly recover their rights politically and socially. This inevitably led to more advanced forms of social struggle. In essence, the wave of reforms was more important for the social forces it unleashed than for its legacy of success fulfillment.

Between October of 1944 and June of 1954, Guatemala experienced almost ten years of euphoria. Juan José Arévalo, an educator and philosopher who preached "spiritual socialism," was elected president in 1945 by a broad political alliance, winning 85 percent of the votes cast. His government set up Social Security in 1946, founded the Indigenous Peoples Institute (Instituto Indigenista), developed public health programs, set forth a Labor Code in 1947, and created a public development corporation in 1948. The new labor organization and the proliferation of union organizations

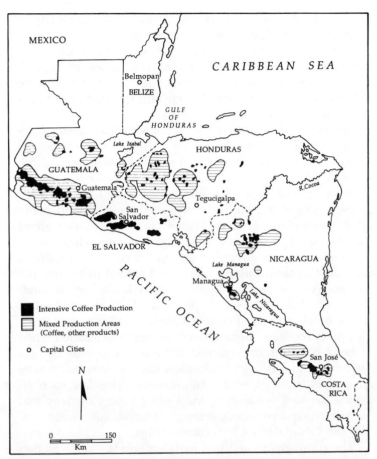

**Map 13.** After World War II coffee production expanded and cultivation was modernized. Nicaragua had become a much more important producer than it had been around 1900. Honduras, without the rich volcanic soils of its neighbors, also succeeds in becoming an exporter. The relative dispersion of coffee-growing areas in both countries, especially Honduras, shows how transportation difficulties frustrated attempts to consolidate production during the latter third of the last century. Basic information came from Nuhn et al. atlas (cited in map 3) from FAO's 1974 *World Coffee Production* (*Estado Mundial del Café*).

provoked confrontations with the United Fruit Company in 1948 and 1949. The coffee plantation owners became very uneasy. Even though the mobilization of the Indian communities was minimal, the agrarian reform law of 1949 allowed some landless peasants to acquire lands thanks to the German-owned plantations the government had seized during World War II.

Arévalo had to face twenty-five attempted military take-overs as well as an insidious press campaign both inside and outside Guatemala. The political scene clouded even further after the mysterious assassination of Colonel Arana, chief of staff of the Army, in 1949. Arana was well-known for his conservative views and was suspected to be behind many of the attempted takeovers. With his death the conservatives had lost their best candidate for the upcoming elections.

Colonel Jacobo Arbenz Guzmán succeeded Arévalo as president in 1951. Internal affairs had tended to become polarized as a result of a more organized reaction by landowners and the more visible presence of unions and leaders of the newly organized (1949) Guatemalan Communist Party. But these conflicts only menaced the regime's stability when Arbenz put forth an Agrarian Reform Act in June of 1952 that was aimed at large landowners holding over 90 hectares [224 acres], and especially fallow lands. This law soon affected the vast holdings of the United Fruit Company that had been acquired mainly through generous concessions under the Estrada and Ubico dictatorships.

The company argued that its fallow lands—some 85 percent of its total landholdings in 1953—in western Guatemala were a safeguard against plagues and diseases of banana trees. The government followed the recommendations of a mission from the IBRD (International Bank for Reconstruction and Development, the predecessor of the World Bank), which considered them vital for a program to promote basic food production, and expropriated the unused lands, compensating the United Fruit Company at its declared aggregate value of slightly over $600,000 dollars. The Company insisted that their real value was in excess of $15,000,000 and appealed to Washington. The adversaries had lined up in an unequal and unjust struggle. United States propaganda attempted to present Guatemala as becoming a Soviet satellite and anti-imperialist outcries inside and outside Guatemala followed the usual pattern. The Archbishop of Guatemala called for an uprising against the "communists" in April and Arbenz purchased arms in Czechoslovakia. The CIA was authorized to organize operation "PBSUCCESS," which consisted of an invasion from Honduras led by two exiled Guatemalan military officers along with an effective propaganda campaign that created confusion inside the government and among the people.

Arbenz stepped down from the presidency on June 27, 1954. The army chose not to resist the invasion while the unions and some political parties had the will to resist but lacked arms and adequate organization to do so. Violence replaced politics and real power passed into the hands of the military.

The Guatemalan regime after 1954 came to be, in this sense, archetypical. The habitual preeminence of the executive branch facilitated the centralization of power by the military while the main source of legitimization became approval by business leaders, legalized political parties, the Church, and the military itself. Under these conditions political participation could only be very restricted with barely any popular backing. Repression, selectively applied, continued remorselessly. It finally became an inseparable part of the regime itself. Political violence was a virtually established rule of the game.

The fall from power of Hernández Martínez in El Salvador in a coup d'etat by the former chief of police, Osmín Aguirre, opened a brief interval of hopefulness that had not been felt since 1944. El Salvador's reformist climate, that began in 1949, was gradual, lacking real achievements, and was initiated under Colonel Osorio's military government. During the 1950s the economic boom created by high coffee prices inspired the development of some health, housing, and social security programs. As might have been expected, the government's emphasis was in developing agricultural diversification and industrial growth that actively fostered private initiative and resulted in heavy investments in infrastructure. The persecution of unions continued and few of the fruits of prosperity trickled down to the lowest rungs. Osorio's political ambitions seem to have been directed at forming an official political party modeled on Mexico's PRI. However, when a military candidate was selected for the 1956 elections, it was obvious that more traditional views still prevailed. El Salvador's regime was clearly becoming increasingly similar to neighboring Guatemala's.

In Honduras, Carías left power in 1948 and the presidency was taken over by an attorney for the banana companies. Dr. Gálvez was not the puppet everyone had expected and managed to develop a moderate modernization. He created the Central Bank, promoted coffee exports, some economic diversification, and improved the network of roads, among other accomplishments. At the end of his term in 1954, the banana workers began a strike and Gálvez, compromised by his complicity in U.S. plans to intervene in Guatemala, did not dare repress it. The strike movement grew, acquired some international backing, and ended up achieving some important victories. The most important of these was legalization of unions. This event paved the way for the adoption of labor legislation in 1957.

Gálvez allowed free elections in 1954 and Ramón Villeda Morales who was the Liberal Party leader won against Tiburcio Carías. But it was not until 1957 after two years of dictatorship and thanks to a military coup led by recently graduated professional officers that the results of the election were respected. Villeda Morales governed until 1963 and enjoyed a broad-based support that included the banana workers union and various middle class and popular groups. He accelerated Gálvez's modernization programs. Villeda Morales tried to attract foreign investment and promote public works and social security. In 1962 he decreed an agrarian reform that clearly reflected the goals of the Alliance for Progress in that it affected only fallow lands. In fact it served

**Map 14.** The expansion of cotton production along the Pacific Coast is shown. For banana plantations, areas in production as well as abandoned areas are indicated. The abandoned areas were initial plantation areas between the end of the nineteenth century and the 1930s. Basic data were extracted from Nuhn et al., atlas, and from West and Augelli, *Middle America*, p. 389.

mainly to expel Salvadorean squatters on Honduran land along the border between the two countries. A military coup ended Villeda Morales' government in 1963. Nonetheless his reform programs were continued but in a more repressive climate.

Nicaragua's Anastasio Somoza García was the only Central American dictator of the 1930s who survived into the postwar period. Having a firm personal control of the National Guard, he proved able to take advantage of the growth of the cotton industry during the 1940s and 1950s and acquired considerable personal benefits. Likewise Somoza was very attentive to the various missions and international organizations through which he discovered wonderful opportunities to develop Nicaragua's infrastructure. For Nicaragua, the state did not as much represent the "will" of "general interests" of the people as it did more and more the interests of the Somoza family itself. When Anastasio Somoza García was shot to death in 1956, Eisenhower sent his own personal physician to cooperate in the fruitless attempts to save his life. Succession to the presidency was assured by his sons: Luis was named president immediately, and Anastasio, chief of the National Guard.

Costa Rica was the only country in which a reform program could enjoy the coherence and political conditions that would allow it to last. Most of these conditions were guaranteed during the civil war of 1948. The pretext for the rebellion was that the government attempted to circumvent the outcome of that year's February elections. The pretext does not reveal much about the real achievements of those critical months in contemporary Costa Rican history. José Figueres Ferrer headed up a movement derived from social democracy. This movement shared some of the thinking of Arévalo in Guatemala during this period and enjoyed some popular support. Arévalo, president of Guatemala, did not deny Figueres support during this critical period. In May of 1948 a junta headed by Figueres took power for eighteen months with the agreement to hand over the government to the winner of the February 1948 elections. That year and a half was sufficient to consolidate a broad program of reforms that were partially enshrined in the new Constitution ratified in 1949. The most visible reform was the elimination of the standing army, which was already inconsequential in military terms. Other reforms were the organizing of the Civil Service and an Elections Tribunal that would guarantee the integrity of future elections. The most fundamental were unquestionably the nationalization of the banking industry, the promotion of cooperativism (embodying many opportunities for small- and medium-sized rural landowners), and the modernization of education and support for social security programs, begun by Calderón Guardia in 1942.

The overall impact of these reforms assured that income was redistributed towards the urban and rural middle sectors. This fact was particularly important when coffee prices were high during the 1950s. Not only could economic and social development in Costa Rica be redefined but it provided as well the basis for continuity in representative democracy and a broadening of political participation.

Despite appearances, the short 1948 civil war and the reformist activities of the ruling junta that was in power for a year and a half had little resemblance to a "revolution from above." The political compromise was part of the settlement of the civil war, and the enactment of changes took place much more slowly than the Social Democratic leaders had anticipated. This was evident in 1949 when the Constituent Assembly set out the new "Magna Carga" for Costa Rica and chose to update the 1871 liberal Constitution rather than undertake the much more radical approach that the Social Democratic delegates were pushing for. The new Constitution was ratified in 1950 when the junta handed over power to president-elect Otilio Ulate who had patiently been waiting since the February 1948 elections to take office.

Fundamental reforms were finally secured during the term of Figueres (1953–1958), the first president elected under the new Constitution, and this was greatly aided by the overwhelming plurality of votes he received. In time, reformist ideas filtered down throughout the whole political spectrum of contemporary Costa Rica. Differences of opinion now were questions of emphasis rather than matters of principle.

The reasons underlying the gradual but continuous success of reformism are to be sought—as we have already argued—in the existence of a diverse and autonomous middle class that was very active socially and politically. Nevertheless, we need to mention other more circumstantial aspects that are no less significant.

José Figueres was an exceptional leader. He had immense personal charisma equaled by exceptional political skills both in the domestic as well as international arenas. He also believed passionately in the reformist principles and in democracy. The Social Democratic reform program exhibited a notable ideological coherence that was due primarily to the creativity of Rodrigo Facio. The reforms were not naive copies of other models but entire reformulations arising from his profound and detailed insight into Costa Rica's reality.

Political alliances and opposition likewise had a major role. The vicissitudes of the 1940s pitted Figueres and his allies against the Communist Party. This conflict lasted throughout the civil war and reached its height when the junta exiled the major opposition leaders and vigorously persecuted unions. That marked anticommunism was very helpful during the 1950s when the Cold War and McCarthyism were most intense by removing any taint of subversiveness from the government. The showdown with the Communist Party had another longer lasting consequence. The country had experienced active unionizing and had achieved certain major reforms during the 1930s and 1940s so that the success of an alternative reformist program implied taking up the same ideas and extending them even further. Figueres and his party pursued this strategy and were conspicuously successful in transplanting these initiatives in all areas of government.

Costa Rican democracy acquired thereby a visible solidness and the country enjoyed significant political stability within a Latin American context. The formal democratic processes were progressively perfected. The national government took on a more active role in balancing vested interests and conflicts between the widest variety of social groups. Even though governmental initiatives in distributing internal wealth reduced incentives for isolated social protest, the workings of the system also involved many informal processes. Two such that continued are the traditional sorts of paternalism and cronyism that are typical of a peasant society in the process of modernization. These processes had the virtue of balancing out some of the undesirable traits of a formal organization or bureaucratic inefficiency. Since these processes depend far more on the individual than the office held, the periodic replacement of officeholders every four years and the alternation of political parties in government become singularly important. They are essential to social equilibrium.

## ECONOMIC CHANGE: INDUSTRIALIZATION AND THE CENTRAL AMERICAN COMMON MARKET

The postwar economic boom spurred modernization and diversification in types of export crops. Coffee received particular attention as might be expected. Improved techniques did not lead to great savings in labor costs, but they did substantially improve the per-hectare production. Banana growers switched from the *Gros Michel* variety that had proven defenseless against pests to the *Cavendish* variety, more resistant but also more delicate to ship. This latter fact led to shipment in boxes that ended up saving shipping space and weight as well as increasing employment. Cotton in the 1950s, beef and sugar in the subsequent decade took their place alongside traditional exports. All this after 1959 helped compensate for the fall in coffee prices, and the economic boom continued in Central America up to the rise in petroleum prices in 1973.

All of this visibly altered the agrarian landscape. By the

end of the 1930s the banana plantations had reached down to the Pacific lowlands in Guatemala (Tiquisate) and Costa Rica (Golfito). Years later the same happened with the cotton fields in El Salvador and Nicaragua. When the traditional cattle industry discovered large profitable export markets in the United States (hamburger meat and different sorts of sausages), the result was a new agricultural expansion throughout all Central America. This was first preceded by the deforestation of vast areas of tropical forests. The penetration even reached into the Atlantic lowlands and the most inaccessible parts of the central highlands. Ecologically, therefore, there was a reassignment of the natural resources. These new export crops displaced traditional grain production to other generally less suitable areas and greatly reduced the virgin topical forests. In one sense, all this signaled in the 1970s the end of a frontier for extensive agricultural expansion. The social consequences were visible first in El Salvador. With its denser population since colonial times and its land area limited to the Pacific slopes, El Salvador was already known in the 1930s for its steady current of migrants into Honduras, particularly the large uninhabited areas on the Honduran frontier with El Salvador. An upsurge in this migratory flow of peasants during the 1960s sparked serious friction between the governments of both countries culminating in the so-called Soccer War that broke out in 1969.

What unquestionably changed the economic and social face of the Isthmus was the industrialization that went along with the creation of *MERCOMUN*, the Central American Common Market (CACM). The General Agreements signed by Guatemala, Honduras, El Salvador, Nicaragua, and Costa Rica in 1960 (Costa Rica did not formally enter until 1963) created a free trade zone, provided fiscal incentives for new industries, and set up several regional organizations. The Central American Bank for Economic Integration (*Banco Centroamericano de Integración Económica*) was a very important channel for financial assistance from the United States for developing infrastructure. Direct private sector investment was especially favored.

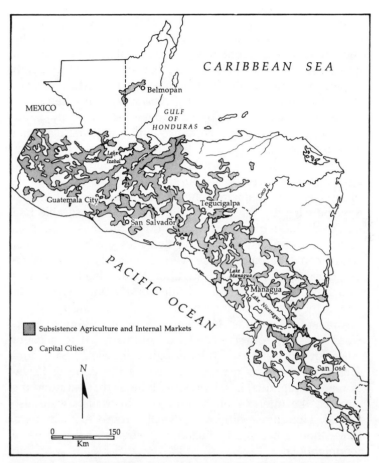

**Map 15.** The map indicates regions producing for local consumption and simplifies estimates by Nuhn et al. in map 3. If this map is viewed in conjunction with a relief map (map 2) and one indicating export production (maps 13 and 14), we can see how production of basic foodstuffs is located in central regions that are frequently more isolated and undeveloped.

Between 1961 and 1969 interregional commerce grew sevenfold. This illustrates the system's initial success. At the same time, overall economic growth revealed average annual growth rates of the GDP (Gross Domestic Product) of about 6 percent. The Economic Commission for Latin America (*CEPAL: Comisión Económica para América Latina*) when it designed CACM in the 1950s had suggested that only a few industries be set up in accordance with a regional plan that took into account the needs and interests of each country. However this latter principle was abandoned by the 1960 agreements because of pressure from U.S. investors. In its place was a more liberal scheme that encompassed almost any industry. By the end of the 1960s the foreseeable had occurred. Industries were concentrated in those countries having the greatest population densities where the lowest wages could be paid. Those were Guatemala and El Salvador. Nicaragua and Costa Rica, after threatening to withdraw from CACM several times, achieved a modus vivendi in which they were able to continue their own industrial development. Honduras, however, was relatively more backward and less cohesive, and this situation led to a major crisis for the country. Even though the 1969 El Salvador–Honduras war was mainly sparked by the issue of Salvadorean immigrants, in the bitter exchanges that led up to the conflict, the interests of Honduran industrialists were also voiced. Honduras withdrew officially from CACM in 1971. Since then it has signed bilateral agreements with some of its neighbors.

In the 1970s it became evident that CACM had become largely obsolete as a viable alternative in development. Industries substituted imports of nondurable consumer goods, but there was an increase in the consumption of raw materials and semi-finished goods. After 1973 in the throes of a world economic crisis, the balance of payments situation worsened progressively. In simpler terms, we could say that the costs of development had become harder and harder to afford.

How can the limitations and impact of industrialization in

Central America be properly evaluated? There are some helpful comparative indices. At the close of the 1970s, some 15 to 20 years after industrialization had been initiated, there was a 40 percent increase in the value-added tax by local industry which was concentrated in the foodstuffs, beverages, and tobacco sector. The chemical industry and the metals-machinery sector contributed less than a 20 percent value-added increase; whereas textiles, a typical branch of light industry, was only of slight significance in Guatemala and El Salvador. All this clearly reveals that Central American industry had a typical process of "import-substitution" in its infancy. Let us note, for instance, that Argentina showed similar increases in value added by industry in the 1900–1929 period whereas between 1925 and 1945 the textiles, transportation, and machinery sectors were the most dynamic.

Yet another feature of Central America's industrialization within the context of CACM has been how early the industrialization process became exhausted. The crisis arose while the process was still just beginning. This is reflected in the growing weight of imports as a percentage of the GDP. In 1980 the percentage varied between about 26 percent in Guatemala and 51 percent in Honduras. We should note that in the cases of Brazil or Argentina when the first major "exhaustion" occurred in the process of industrialization during the 1960s, the value of imports as a percentage of the GDP hovered around 5 percent.

Among the most negative impacts of industrialization in Central America has been employment. The percentage of the population actively involved in industry was constant between 1950 and 1972, about 10 percent. It is estimated that between 1958 and 1972 economic integration created some 150,000 jobs, both direct and indirect. This represents about 3 percent of the total labor force and about 14 percent of the overall increase in the labor force if we combine all five Central American nations.

Did, then, CACM and industrialization represent the best economic choice for Central America during the 1960s? The answer is certainly affirmative for the local business communities and for foreign investors. There are also strong arguments in favor of economic integration from the perspective of the size of the regional market and profitability. However the early "exhaustion" of the industrialization process and inability to advance to the next phase of "substitution," apparent during the 1970s, led to serious doubts: not doubts about the value of integration in and of itself— these are undeniable—but doubts concerning the direction and means that industrialization actually took. In 1972, SIECA (*PERMANENT SECRETARIAT OF THE AGREEMENT FOR ECONOMIC INTEGRATION IN CENTRAL AMERICA*) published a gloomy report in which it warned of the necessity for profound internal changes, particularly in agriculture, and the urgency of bringing about better planning and coordination between the governments to allow industrial growth to continue.

A general perusal of the numerous documents generated by international organizations and some government statistics leads to the impression that the overall cost of industrialization has been borne by the great majority of the population whereas its greatest benefits have been enjoyed by a narrow group of business owners and middle sectors. Only in Costa Rica have these general effects been greatly attenuated. This has been due to the systematic intervention by the government and to the consistent process of reform. True, this was achieved at the price of a huge increase in public expenditures, growing external debt, and a growing trade deficit.

Urbanization suffered a change of character. The Central American capitals went from sleepy small towns with their provincial simplicity to the agitated lifestyle of modern cities. Increasing numbers of marginal poor, lack of basic services and dwellings, and increasing crime are all among the many varied outcomes of the fast growth of cities. Nearby small towns were swallowed up by the growth of the capitals into new metropolitan entities whose areas grew in proportion to their lack of planning. These urban centers were in any case linked together by certain salient traits: agglomerations of the poor into shanty towns, new industries, or newly built highways.

Internal migrations, caused as much by rapid population growth as by changes in the rural setting, fed this new environment. Socially their consequences were overwhelming: new attitudes and customs changed forever the traditional patterns of rural life. There were dramatically new political realities. In this new urban environment, mobilization and protest soon took on a frequently explosive character.

## POLITICS AND SOCIETY: CRISIS OF THE LIBERAL ORDER

By the 1960s, there were signs of a crisis in the old liberal order, which had come into being a century earlier. Social protests had become increasingly difficult to contain and growing repression was the response of the ruling classes to pressures for social change. These pressures included guerrilla movements in Guatemala and Nicaragua. Handing over power to the military became more and more necessary to assure survival of the landowners and business leaders who stubbornly regarded every attempt at social justice as part of a conspiracy controlled now not from Moscow but from Castro's Havana. In essence, this "imminent and menacing conspiracy" was no more than an ideological coverup of an undeniable fact: the system of social relations based on exclusion, created during the liberal reforms of the last quarter of the nineteenth century, was simply bankrupt.

United States policy had an astonishing duality throughout this whole period. Technical experts and study missions were unequivocally aware of the need for structural changes and reforms. Nonetheless in the end, the hand of the U.S. State Department always obeyed strategic considerations. This is why there was unconditional support for all the region's repressive regimes, such as that given to Somoza. These strategic considerations were characterized by a mixture of ignorance and disregard for the legitimate ambitions of the great majority of the Central Americans. There was also the voracity of certain U.S. businesses that had the willing ear of Washington's official circles.

Kennedy's Alliance for Progress, organized in 1961, intended to push forward economic growth, certain structural changes (especially in agriculture), and democratization in politics. Behind those ambitious reforms lay hidden in reality a counterinsurgency operation using modernization and practical democracy. The effort was to reverse the Cuban Revolution and the guerrilla movements that threatened to multiply wherever there were fertile conditions. However that enormous test of the virtues of capitalism versus the menacing promises of socialism soon failed. The ruling classes resisted and sabotaged most of the social reforms; at the same time they derived benefits from their growing association with U.S. investors and the investment capital that flowed so generously during the prosperous 1960s. Armies and the police were rearmed and modernized. Internal repression now became increasingly effective and its success against the guerrilla struggle was unmistakable. By around 1970 subversion in Nicaragua and Guatemala had been sufficiently hard hit and was no longer very threatening. More important was that subversion seemed blocked in the nick of time in El Salvador and Honduras. It mattered little—against the context of the Vietnam War—that the goals of democracy and popular elections, part of the sophisticated original plan, had become shelved awaiting a more opportune moment. Essentially, the specter of a subversive threat was such a successful tactic for the military and ruling classes that it was not wise to provoke them into invoking it.

The Church, traditionally a pillar of conservatism, began to behave in frequently contradictory ways, such as is typical of a corporate body. The first example was the behavior of Bishop Sanabria in Costa Rica during the 1940s that proved important in getting social reforms adopted and in helping the labor movement. Another more recent instance originates from different branches of the Church, or organizations related to it, in El Salvador, Guatemala, Honduras, and

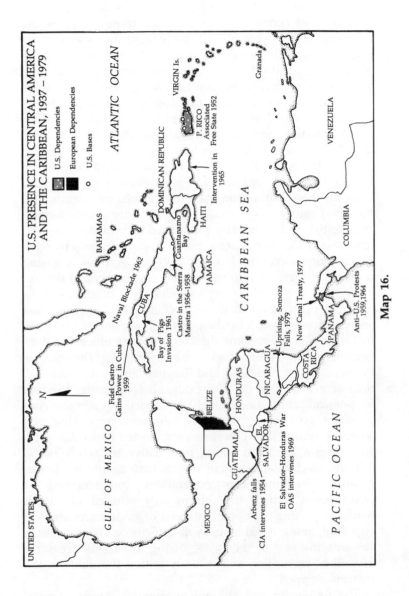

**U.S. PRESENCE IN CENTRAL AMERICA AND THE CARIBBEAN, 1937–1979**

U.S. Dependencies

European Dependencies

o   U.S. Bases

ATLANTIC OCEAN

UNITED STATES

GULF OF MEXICO

N

BAHAMAS

Fidel Castro Gains Power in Cuba 1959

Naval Blockade 1962

CUBA

Bay of Pigs Invasion 1961

Castro in the Sierra Maestra 1956–1958

JAMAICA

Guantanamo Bay

HAITI

DOMINICAN REPUBLIC

Intervention in 1965

P. RICO Associated Free State 1952

VIRGIN Is.

CARIBBEAN SEA

MEXICO

Arbenz falls CIA intervenes 1954

GUATEMALA

BELIZE

HONDURAS

EL SALVADOR

El Salvador–Honduras War OAS intervenes 1969

NICARAGUA

Uprising, Somoza Falls, 1979

COSTA RICA

New Canal Treaty, 1977

PANAMA

Anti–U.S. Protests 1959,1964

PACIFIC OCEAN

Granada

VENEZUELA

COLUMBIA

**Map 16.**

Nicaragua. The work in the (religious) communities, the organization of cooperatives and diverse forms of grassroots associations were possible initially because they sprang from an institution "above all suspicion" in the eyes of repressive forces. In almost all cases, these activities were begun as alternatives to the "Communist Menace." The results were clearly unforeseen owing to the dynamics of these Church organizations and associations which soon had to face injustice, reaction, and violence. And then there were the profound changes in Church leadership after Vatican II.

The military were also sometimes inclined to take up the banner of sincere reforms. But since they were limited to carrying them out within state and institutional authority, they had rather less success. In El Salvador a new moderately leftist civilian-military junta tried to provide a new alternative in October of 1960, but it was overthrown by rightist military forces in January of 1961. Another uprising occurred in 1972 as a protest against corruption and the imposition of the official party's candidate as president along with the open fraud in those elections. This uprising was soon suppressed with the help of the Guatemalan Air Force. In Guatemala itself, some dissident military officers took to guerrilla warfare themselves at the beginning of the 1960s as in the cases of Yon Sosa and Turcios Lima. In Honduras, the fragmentation of the ruling class allowed greater freedom for political action. López Arellano headed a repressive conservative government between 1963 and 1970. However, when he returned to power in 1972, he felt noticeable pressure from a group of young progressive military officers. This resulted in an agrarian reform that distributed lands, organized peasants into cooperatives, and arranged for credit. Even though the reform only affected idle land, hardly impacting the vested interests of landowners and foreign companies, it did assure self-sufficiency in basic grains. Towards the end of the 1970s, owing to various pressures as well as corruption and disunity within the military, the reforms stopped.

The university and student movements deserve special

consideration. One achievement of the wave of reforms after World War II was the autonomy of the universities. This autonomy converted them into potential seedbeds of opposition. Except for Costa Rica, their relations with governmental authorities became clearly strained. The universities did not escape direct intervention by the government (El Salvador in 1972) or selective bloody interventions as in Guatemala since 1970. Regardless of this, student movements and the universities often enjoyed a certain marginal freedom to act, and in some cases they made themselves heard and became very active. Their most significant role without a doubt has been to help develop a critical consciousness towards national problems within different segments of ruling groups. Student movements have been key elements of solidarity with protests of various sorts from street demonstration to propaganda and other types of agitation. Maintaining a continually vigorous opposition has been perhaps the most singular trait of the universities and student movements in Guatemala, Honduras, El Salvador, and Nicaragua.

The transformative role of political parties has been reduced in the context of limited democracy. Excepting Costa Rica, elections never resulted in handing over power to the opposition unless there were heavy restrictions attached. "Preventative" coups to avoid elections or giving an electoral winner the presidency, open electoral fraud, highly controlled electoral campaigns with barely any opposition, a "pact" within the ruling oligarchy that envisaged a limited or restricted access to governmental power were all typical mechanisms of Central American politics during this period. Only the Guatemalan elections of 1944 and 1950 and those in Honduras in 1957 actually resulted in a clean, unrestricted handing over of power.

Despite all this, electoral campaigns opened up a margin for political struggle and for varied displays of opposition. This margin of political expression was demonstrably supported by the Alliance for Progress and by some newly formed "modern" political parties, ones not associated with the strongman tradition (caudillismo) but having a rather solid ideological base. The parties that represented an important political innovation in this context were the Christian Democrats, the Social Democrats, and the refurbishing of some traditional parties upon new foundations. Of the latter the most notable was the Honduran Liberal Party after Villeda Morales. These new political forces, some of which had international ties, were able to make use of a wider scope of reference as well as some protective cover in decrying abuse, arbitrary actions, and atrocities, all of which have come increasingly to characterize Central American political life.

However we choose to look at it, guerrilla movements were an especially significant new element in the welter of political forces and social change. Two phases are clearly delineated. In the first, during the 1960s, guerrilla groups that sprang up in Guatemala and Nicaragua were successfully controlled by counterinsurgency strategies inaugurated under the auspices of the Alliance for Progress. As might have been expected, volunteerism and individual heroics were not enough to incite the rural masses to revolt. The reaction of the ruling classes tended to be, in all the countries, more and more unified. Thus organizations, such as CONDECA (Central American Defense Counsel), with U.S. military help, were fundamental. CONDECA was a product of a treaty between the armed forces of Guatemala, Honduras, and Nicaragua in 1963. El Salvador signed in 1965 and Panama in 1973; Costa Rica entered symbolically in 1966. Anastasio Somoza Debayle's role was not unsupportive of the unification process. His enduring and seemingly solid political and military power in Nicaragua were a sort of security against the often volatile ups and downs of Central American politics. The need for such security became rather evident, at the time of the Honduran–Salvadorean war of 1969 with its openly nationalist overtones or when the Torrijos military dictatorship started a persistent struggle to assert Panamanian sovereignty over the Canal (especially between 1969 and 1977).

The second phase, in the 1970s, shows quite another character. Insurrection succeeded in establishing a solid popular base in Nicaragua and El Salvador, while in Guatemala the guerrilla movement reached out to the Indian masses. Somoza's fall in July of 1979 marks the high point of this new phase. It was quickly followed by another coup d'etat in El Salvador that same year which was a clear response to the growing successes of the Salvadorean guerrillas. How did this new situation come about? What is the basis for this broad grassroots mobilization? We will attempt at least to sketch an answer.

The several versions of the failure of reform led ineluctably to a tragic and drastic social and political oversimplification. A strike or simple demands for justice by workers became with astonishing rapidity a social protest with much broader repercussions. Nothing happened without recourse to mobilizing diverse social groups: unions, student organizations, the Church, and so forth. Repression, which had been the habitual response by the state and ruling classes, also began to affect a broader group. In essence, the conflict was not confined to institutional or political channels and this was one of the costs of the failure of reforms. Any sort of protest, no matter how timid, questioned the system itself and was seen as part of a subversive conspiracy. The endless chain of exclusions that inevitably extended to political opposition resulted finally in another equally implacable consequence: a permanent questioning of the established order by social groups as broad-based as they were varied.

Still, it is obvious that a generalized insurrection having strong support among the rural masses did not simply follow the escalating reaction by the ruling class. This was very evident in El Salvador. On the one hand, there was a culturally homogeneous peasantry that was quite proletarianized and had high population density. Although industrial workers were in a minority, the population of marginal urban poor soon became quite large. On the other hand, the 1969 war with Honduras closed the door to the easiest sort of peasant migration thereby shutting off a traditional "escape valve" used by the numerous rural landless and unemployed peasant laborers. Other factors, such as the Cerrón Grande hydroelectric dam, finished in 1977, created further expropriations and displacement of large groups of the rural population. Within this context, the impact of various guerrilla organizations, who had begun to operate as small isolated groups since 1971, took on unusual dimensions with a speed nothing short of explosive. To be precise, the ranks of the guerrillas were continually swelled by the repressive measures themselves, measures that the military and various paramilitary groups carried out. Persecution and death fell heavily upon priests, students, politicians, labor leaders, and peasants: in short, on anyone having real or possible links with clandestine organizations. The 1979 military takeover was an effort, clearly favored by U.S. interests and the Carter administration, to break the hellish circle of repression, death, and revolt.

Nicaragua offers a very different example. The Somoza family's power grew to such an extent, especially after the 1972 earthquake that destroyed Managua, that it threatened the vested interests of local business itself. Consider, for example, that by 1979 the Somoza family possessed one-third of all the assets in the Nicaraguan economy. This, along with having opposition leader Pedro Joaquín Chamorro assassinated, brought about a truly unified front of the classes against the Somoza dynasty. This situation reinvigorated and gave new social support to the Sandinista Front, a guerrilla movement from the 1960s. The success in 1979 of this dramatic struggle of the people against state power, which cost over 40,000 lives, cannot be understood without also taking into account international factors. The inconsistent U.S. policy under Carter all of a sudden found itself without allies or choices in deciding between unconditional support for the crumbling dynasty or amoral stance on human rights. The Sandinista Front received abundant help from such important neighbors as Mexico, Venezuela, and Cuba along with others that were strategically situated such as Panama and Costa Rica. The progressive international rejection of the Somoza regime allowed the formation of an opposition that was as varied as it was effective just as was happening within Nicaragua.

Guatemala's guerrilla movement was practically destroyed in 1970 after it had enjoyed some spectacular successes in the cities but had completely failed in operation in the countryside. Nonetheless, the guerrillas reappeared in 1975 now showing strong support in the central and eastern highlands. The growth in guerrilla activity in the subsequent years demonstrated unequivocally one thing: indigenous communities were now politically mobilized and had come to be one of the bases of support for the insurrection. How did such a radical change take place? The answer lies in the growing economic and cultural "fragmentation" of the Indian communities. These communities were impacted by capitalist expansion and population increase. Added to these factors are the actions of the Catholic Church and several Protestant sects. These are at least some of the decisive factors accounting for the rapid growth of conscientiousness. We should not lose track, however, of the ethnic diversity and the size of the area affected, with its regional differences and significant natural barriers to communication, which are serious obstacles to the eventual success of an insurrection.

Against this panorama of deep crisis, Costa Rica revealed very different features. The challenges that arose in the 1970s were answered by extended reforms. Social Security was amplified to the point where it was virtually universal. In the area of agrarian reform, an active plan of settlement managed to contain growing pressure for land in some parts of the country. Perhaps the most decisive step was the attempt, financed by a short rise in coffee prices during 1976 and 1977, to promote a complex of industries of mixed ownership involving both the state and private sectors. However, corruption and inefficiency, together with a dramatic shift in national policy between 1978 and 1982 quickly undercut these reforms.

The triumph of Nicaragua's popular revolt and an upsurge in El Salvador's insurrection constitute perhaps a turning point in the Isthmus's history. In any case they represent a rethinking of U.S. influence in the area that ought to be regarded as equivalent to the Soviet presence in Cuba or the new Canal Zone treaties signed in Panama in 1977. The strategic importance of the Isthmus arises again since its conflicts are now viewed in the context of a confrontation between East and West. This is all very obvious from the perspective of the chess game of international politics. But it is extremely unjust and limited if one honestly considers the deep causes of the insurrection.

# 6

# The Present Crisis (1980–1987)

Crisis is the order of the day. There is no better way to characterize Central America in the first half of this decade. The word "crisis" permeates the news, turns up unavoidably in daily conversations, is shrieked out in street demonstrations. It pours fear into many and shakes people quickly out of their innocence. Still, aside from collective psychology, is there an objective basis for today's crises?

The economic morass is circumscribed within the long continuing worldwide economic recession. The signs are unmistakable.[1] The Gross Domestic Product's growth rate has steadily slowed and in 1982 the five countries even experienced a negative growth. On a per capita basis, the situation seems even worse. Between 1980 and 1984 per capita production declined by 10 percent in Costa Rica and Nicaragua, by some 15 percent in Guatemala, and by over 20 percent in Honduras and El Salvador. Similar symptoms can be seen in the persistent deficit in current balance of payments between 1978 and 1983. In 1983, the indices revealed a 30 to 40 percent drop relative to 1977. The increase in foreign indebtedness has not been any less dramatic. It has increased fourfold between 1977 and 1983. Inflation, unemployment, and currency devaluation illustrate from other vantage points how critical the situation has become. Medium-term forecasts are hardly reassuring. None of the Central American countries can meet their foreign debt payments without a clear recovery in the international economy, especially a substantial increase in export prices.

The common character of the crisis phenomenon among all five Central American countries leads us to suspect that internal social and political factors are only aggravating circumstances and not causes. Costa Rica and, to a lesser de-

gree, Honduras, have enjoyed a singular political and governmental stability in comparison with Nicaragua, El
Salvador, and Guatemala, all of which have been afflicted
with civil wars and violence. The economic crisis, however,
pardons no country. Given that the shakeup in the world
economy has coincided with the clear exhaustion of industrial development within the Central American Common
Market, the export crisis has brought about a severe general
economic crisis just as had happened in earlier periods.

The ruins of the Central American Common Market
(CACM) have deeper meaning. They are not just the result
of wrong timing with respect to outside markets, of bad business decisions, or misdirected development policies. Much
more than all these, they show the failure of a development
model that has been incapable of breaking through structural
barriers to social progress. It is therefore impossible to imagine that the crisis will be eliminated with a simple world
economic recovery. To overcome this crisis implies that development options be reoriented. There are two alternatives,
not mutually exclusive, that emerge with some clarity: (1) a
radical redefinition of regional integration including other
countries within the Caribbean basin; and (2) new strategies
of linking with the world market involving a major diversification in exports and the opening up of new markets.

In sociopolitical terms, we are frankly talking about the
bankruptcy of a model of social control: the Liberal order
imposed a century ago. But expressing it in this apparently
simple way actually hides an extraordinary complexity.

The political crisis is in one sense an internal matter that
can only be appreciated properly on the basis of a detailed
study of each country's own situation. But the changes that
have taken place, such as El Salvador's and Guatemala's civil
war or the building of a new social order as in Sandinista
Nicaragua, have radically affected the status quo of international relations throughout the whole area.

The diminishing U.S. hegemony and the active presence
of new interests imply not only regional conflict and redefinition. The conflicts that have been unleashed have even

caused two extreme situations: the contingency of direct U.S. military intervention (their October 1983 invasion of the small Caribbean island of Grenada might be regarded as a prelude to a much larger scale operation), and the serious threat of war between two or more Central American nations. Tensions rose to the point that, in January of 1983, Colombia, Mexico, Venezuela, and Panama collectively formed the so-called Contadora group to achieve peace diplomatically. Even though long and complex negotiations did not yield a general peace agreement, the group did manage to avoid what seemed destined to become an imminent armed confrontation.

After Somoza's fall, and especially since the start of the Reagan administration in 1981, U.S. policy has developed along four different fronts. First, setting up military bases in Honduras has transformed that country into an important chip in U.S. defense. Ongoing military maneuvers and a sizeable arsenal built up in Honduras have intimidated the Sandinista government. Furthermore, the U.S. provides rearguard support to the Salvadorean army in its war against the guerrillas and crucial protection for the Contras operating from the Honduran border against the Managua government. Second, there has been increasing U.S. financial and logistic support for anti-Sandinista groups. Third, there was a short episode of direct negotiations with Managua—the talks in Manzanillo in 1984—and support, perhaps only rhetorical, for certain sorts of dialogue between the warring parties, such as those initiated in El Salvador in October of 1984. Fourth, there has been an effort to reformulate an overall policy towards the Central American nations. This is the fundamental idea behind the Caribbean Basin Initiative enacted by the U.S. Congress in July 1983 and behind the *Kissinger Report* of January 1984.

The Caribbean Basin Initiative is a combination of financial incentives seeking closer integration of the area's countries into the U.S. markets. The *Kissinger Report*, on the other hand, has more ambitious objectives. It is a diagnosis of the critical situation in Central America, how that affects U.S.

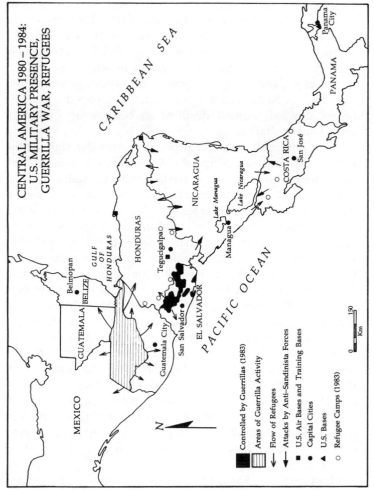

**Map 17.**

interests, and recommendations on formulating an overall policy that can rely upon broad political support in the United States. The latter part is perhaps the report's most far-reaching goal.

The initiative can be quickly summarized. Almost 4,000 products originating in Central America, Panama, Belize, Surinam, Guyana, and the Caribbean islands (excepting Cuba and the French Antilles) will be allowed into U.S. markets duty free for a period of twelve years. Even though textiles, footwear, and leather goods, tuna, and oil are excluded from this list, the allowed products are sufficiently wide-ranging to theoretically enable rapid recovery and export diversification in the region. Too much optimism, however, is hardly realistic. In small national economies with fragmented markets, which lack business experience and skilled labor, and have an inefficient state bureaucracy, it is utopian to expect an early positive response to such incentives. In other words, it seems very unlikely that local businesses will be really capable of meeting this sort of challenge. We should observe, also, that there are many uncertainties within the initiative itself. A nation can be ruled "ineligible" or dropped from "eligibility" for purely political reasons at the discretion of the U.S. president (for example, expropriation of U.S. citizens' property or subsidies to export industries). Furthermore, the space of twelve years for the export incentives to be in force seems too short especially if we consider that they arise from a traditionally protectionist nation.

Accordingly, multinational companies will probably be the prime beneficiaries from the initiative. Only they have in-depth knowledge of U.S. markets, the required technology, and the political influence to prevail against the aforementioned uncertainties. This is not to say that some nations and some local businesses will not achieve major success from the plan. However, it is hard to believe that this plan will be a true alternative development strategy in the long run.

The *Kissinger Report* is based on an analysis of the crisis in Central America that can be summarized as asserting that poverty, repression, and inequalities have deep roots internally within the region, but that they have been cruelly exploited by an imported insurrection from outside the region (Cuba and the Soviet Union). The latter circumstance is a serious threat to U.S. security. Suggested remedies are of two sorts: (1) ample economic aid accompanied by certain social reforms, and (2) a major plan for military assistance. The first includes an $8 billion aid package over a five-year span along with major grants and technical assistance. Although the size of the aid package is very large, it should be noted that the plan is for the funds to be channeled directly into the private sector without local government participation of the recipient country. This may be to avoid corruption—an unhappy memory from the Alliance for Progress—but it also implies contempt for national political authority, the final consequences of which are hard to foresee.

Militarily, the report ratifies the policy line followed by the Reagan administration: increased military aid to El Salvador and Honduras, a curtain around Nicaragua, approval of destabilizing actions against the regime in Managua, "containment" of the Cuba-Soviet menace in the whole area.

The bipartisan character of the commission that produced the report along with its impeccable rhetoric about negotiation, aid, injustice, and military security have insured that it will be influential in efforts to achieve a broad consensus in the United States for Republican policy toward Central America. This consensus was visible in the ninety-seventh U.S. Congress and was reflected as well in Reagan's easy 1984 electoral victory. In 1985 and 1986, after several unsuccessful attempts, the Reagan Administration also managed to get Congress to approve a large economic aid package for the Contras. However, other events have shown that a new policy towards Central America has still not been completely built and we can see several inconsistencies. The secret arms sales to Iran in which the funds earned were used to help the Contras and which became public in November 1986 reflect more than duplicity. They also bring into question the credibility of public declarations, not to mention that of the entire Central American policy issue. With the Democratic Party gaining a majority in the Congressional elections of 1986, we will see at least a fundamental reconsideration, even if no sweeping changes, of U.S. Central American policies. From a U.S. viewpoint, the dilemma that opened up in 1979 with the Sandinistas is still unresolved and includes such questions as what posture to take vis-à-vis a disliked Nicaraguan regime; what to do about the danger of growing insurrection in El Salvador (and eventually Guatemala); what to do about the real or possible increase in Soviet and Cuban influence throughout the region—all without repeating the risks inherent in another Vietnam.

Economic crisis and the international repercussions of sociopolitical change affect with a broad brush the whole of Central America. The same is true of the uncertainties and hopes that are profiled against a gloomy future. Before looking in depth at this future, it will pay us to return to the heart of the crisis and consider in detail the peculiarities of each nation's evolution.

## DISPARITIES AMONG THE NATIONS

In March 1982, General Ríos Montt took over in Guatemala with the classic military coup. Neither its carefully planned execution, nor the prior approval of the U.S. Embassy, nor even the fact that the loser was another military officer were novelties. The escalating repression, economic difficulties, and open fraud in the presidential elections, held only a few days before, had finally extinguished all pretense to the legitimacy of the regime, such as General Romeo Lucas García's had been. He had himself been installed by a similar electoral charade in 1978. No, it was the way the 1982 coup's leaders talked that hinted at originality. Ríos Montt denounced the "death squads" and promised to respect human rights as part of his policy of "guns and beans" ("fusiles y frijoles"). It soon became very apparent, however, that this novel rhetoric hid an equally new counterinsurgency strategy. Old repressive tactics were to be revived to take on the broad-based insurrection that had spread solidly into the Indian communities towards the close of the 1970s.

Military operations continued to carry out wholesale killings within Indian communities. The first, in Panzos, took place in 1978. In 1981 there was evidence of at least twelve similar slaughters. Additionally, there were large-scale forced migrations of Indians. Guerrilla groups soon withdrew and the defenseless Indians, without arms or combat experience, were easy prey for extermination. On top of all this, "strategic hamlets" and civil patrols were set up to control the peasants, who were now moved to "sanitized" areas. The outcome has been a true genocide of several ethnic groups and an immense stream of refugees inside the country and across the Honduran and Mexican borders. The number of refugees has been estimated to have reached 1 million.

In October 1983, Ríos Montt was replaced by yet another coup. Again the changes in the political scene are insignificant. Ríos Montt's fundamentalist Protestant associations quickly led him into conflict with the Catholic Church hierarchy. His reluctance to call for elections inspired a lack of confidence within the U.S. State Department. Similarly his constant references to an agrarian reform program giving lands to the peasants forced into the strategic hamlets along with his avid denunciation of corruption—never more than rhetorical—succeeded in making landowners and the traditional sector of the military, itself involved in repression, very nervous. The new President, General Mejía Victores, lifted the state of siege, promised to restore "democracy" and continue, in close alliance with Washington, the struggle against communism. Policies had returned to a more traditional mold. The 1984 elections for a Constituent Assembly confirm this change and cannot but remind us of the equally critical events that anticipated the presidential elections of 1958 and 1966.

In both of those elections, presidential power was handed

over to a harmless opposition that, by then, lacked any reformist ambitions and was rigidly bound within the legal
framework of the 1956 and 1965 constitutions respectively.
General Ydígoras Fuentes who won in 1958 was an old-style
conservative who had had his initial military experience under the protective wings of Ubico. Ydígoras Fuentes managed to combine with some ingenuity variable degrees of
corruption, paternalism, and repression. It was not enough,
as could have been foreseen, to assure lasting political stability. The 1963 electoral campaign finally precipitated the
crisis. He allowed Arévalo to return amidst a growing popular mobilization. The consequent coup was quickly forthcoming. The old general was replaced by a hardline colonel
and history repeated itself. Once again a Constituent Assembly was convoked and at the close of electoral campaigns
marked by terror and crackdowns the opposition won the
presidency in 1966. This time there was a secret pact that
transformed the elected Méndez Montenegro into a virtual
puppet of the military.

The similarity in the situations remains surprising. Just
as in 1958 and 1966, the outcome in 1985 was a presidential
election held under a new constitution, with the opposition,
now the Christian Democrats, winning. The new president,
Vinicio Cerezo, took office in January of 1986. His favorable
image internationally and his respected political abilities
have assured that the beginning months of his presidency
will enjoy some room for maneuvering in the very difficult
social and economic situation facing Guatemala. But the
power of the military continues to be the decisive one and
is exercised officially through the National Inter-Agency Co-
ordinating Office (Coordinadora Inter-Institucional Nacional)
set up within each province in the country. These advisory
bodies, reporting to the regional military commander, are
integrated into the civilian agencies as well and are the final
authority in each region of the country.

The new government might be able to enact a very moderate program of reforms especially if it can get the necessary
international financial aid and the support of some of the

military. However, it is very hard to see this coming about without a broad grassroots movement and some restoration of civil rights. If all this does take place, there will again be a cycle of violence possibly even worse than the one experienced only a few years ago. This image of a "frozen" society can again be seen in recent Salvadorean history.

In El Salvador, the overall situation presents some newer and perhaps more dramatic features. The coup of 1979 originated in factors both inside and outside the country. The cornerstone lay in the guerrillas' successes and the popular uprising. When the Sandinistas took over in July 1979 in Nicaragua, some Salvadorean groups were fearful, others ebullient. General Romero's regime had exhibited an ineffectiveness that was matched only by the degree to which his repressive policies were repudiated. The coup united heterogeneous groups whose unity was based on political events rather than on shared medium- or long-range goals. Some of the military, some forward-looking business leaders, Christian Democrat, and Social Democrat groups all banded together with the approval of the Catholic Church— a respected and biting critic of the previous regime—and the guarded blessing of the U.S. Embassy.

The new government focused on three separate areas: (1) restoration of the rule of law by removing hardline groups from the military and by eliminating paramilitary squads; (2) either setting free or accounting for the political prisoners and hundreds of "disappeared" persons; (3) designing a daring reform package in response to legitimate popular demands for social justice, thereby co-opting slogans from various guerrilla groups. Within a few months, however, it was clear that while the coup's leaders ran the government, they did not control all the power centers. With a blistering swiftness the ruling class and a significant segment of the military had orchestrated a violent reactionary wave of repression.

There was no removal of hardline groups, nor was any accounting for the "disappeared" forthcoming. In January and February of 1980 it was quite clear that the "death squads" operated freely and had even claimed some government officials as their victims. The nationalization of foreign trade and the banking industry as well as agrarian reform were enacted paradoxically at the beginning of March of that year during the height of a wave of repression that culminated on March 24 with the assassination of the archbishop of San Salvador, Monsignor Oscar Arnulfo Romero. By this time an important political realignment had occurred. The Social Democrats and some factions of the Christian Democrats had left the government and allied themselves in April with other leftist political groups to create the FDR (Revolutionary Democratic Front), the political arm of grassroots organizing and of the guerrilla forces. The Christian Democratic Party, now with its leaders' ranks greatly diminished, entered the government officially. What happened next obeyed an inexorably clear logic.

Repression descended upon grassroots organizations in the urban areas and eliminated all forms of political opposition. All FDR leaders were kidnapped and assassinated during November of that year. By then the guerrilla forces had deployed themselves in the countryside under a unified military command, the FMLN (Farabundo Marti National Liberation Front). The Salvadorean army was counting on increased U.S. military aid. The Christian Democrats within the government were testing a "reforms plus repression" formula. However, the "reforms" part of their formula proved to be more difficult than had been imagined.

The ruling class reacted with virulent opposition to any "reforms." The military was inclined to favor reforms provided the military itself were to benefit economically. A new chain of corruption was forged, while reforms having the greatest popular impact were skillfully delayed or simply erased. All this was particularly visible during 1982–1984 when the Constituent Assembly, elected in March 1982, was dominated by extreme right political parties and deliberately sabotaged reforms, blocked the second stage of agrarian reform, and put the Christian Democrats themselves in a serious bind. Only pressure from the United States prevented an even greater step backward.

Under these circumstances, the impact of reforms could only be very limited. Nationalization of the banking industry and of foreign trade provided the government with major new powers, but their grassroots impact relied heavily on political decisions. Even when such decisions could be reached, the gravity of the economic crisis limited the impact. Agrarian reform, on the other hand, promised to yield more far-reaching results.

The first stage of agrarian reform was aimed at landholdings over 500 hectares [1,250 acres] amounting to 15 percent of the total agricultural holdings and planned to expropriate and distribute over 300 plots. Estimates suggested that some 178,000 workers and family members would benefit. The peasants would be organized into cooperatives and could rely on the assistance and financial aid of ISTA (Salvadorean Institute for Agrarian Transformation). However, transferring titles correctly and getting a cooperative working properly require time and quite a few bureaucratic procedures. By the end of 1982 scarcely twenty titles had been adjudicated definitively. The next stage of reform, yet to begin, will be aimed at landholdings of between 100 and 500 hectares [250 and 1,250 acres]. The third stage applies to farmers wishing to claim title of the land they worked, up to an area of 7 hectares [16.5 acres]. Although 1982 saw the provisional distribution of over 30,000 titles of this sort, the way legislation has been applied and modified by the Constituent Assembly has been full of difficulties and delays. David Browning estimates that between 60,000 and 150,000 peasants would potentially benefit from this third stage. However he also points out: "Agrarian reform alone cannot satisfy the needs of those who have no land."[2] The second stage (still in limbo) is even more problematical. It would impact the most profitable and technically sophisticated agricultural operations and seriously compromise the stability of the exporting sector. This in turn would lead to a virtual economic catastrophe for El Salvador in the short and intermediate run.

The most negative side of agrarian reform has unques-

tionably been the repressive political environment in which
it occurs. There are two aspects that can be highlighted. On
the one hand, the extreme right has victimized through in-
timidation and murder countless persons, even including
U.S. advisors and high officials of the ISTA. The military,
on the other hand, is associated with carrying out reforms,
since without its direct support very little if anything can be
achieved. The price paid is not only seen in corruption,
which has been widely denounced, but also in converting
reform into another counterinsurgency tactic. It is very
doubtful that a parcel of land acquired under these conditions—in the middle of a fratricidal war—could be hailed as
a democratic achievement or a meaningful advance for human dignity.

Land for all does not seem to be a very realistic option,
given El Salvador's available economic resources regardless
of the particular government. A really meaningful change,
benefiting the great majority, should include a major increase in available jobs, a substantial rise in real personal
earnings, social and labor guarantees, and an efficient social
security system.

Realignments in the government occurred between March
of 1980 and June of 1984. They reflect with impeccable clarity
the strength and development of the forces in conflict. By
the end of 1980, Colonel Majano had left the governing
junta. He was a committed albeit a naive reformist who had
participated since the beginning in the coup of October 1979.
Majano's fall and the naming of Napoleón Duarte, a Christian Democrat, as provisional president reveal as much about
the power of the old guard military (in the person of Defense
Minister General García) as of the continuous influence of
the U.S. Embassy. In March of 1982 elections were held for
the Constituent Assembly that appointed a provisional government. The outcome was unexpected. The Christian Democrats only won a relative majority. This implied that the
extreme right parties wielded decisive power in the Assembly. These parties won the ministerial posts of Economy,
Agriculture, and Foreign Trade all of which are key to carry-

ing out any reform program. Duarte won the 1984 presidential elections, but the right coalition continued to hold legislative power until 1985. United States support seems more indispensable than ever to assure him the loyalty of senior military officers and to stay in power.

The other end of the spectrum are the guerrilla movements. The grassroots organizations that had arisen semi-clandestinely from 1972 to 1975 were decimated and virtually vanished between March and November of 1980. Street demonstrations, strikes, and sit-ins were savagely and efficiently quelled. As we said before, the guerrilla forces redeployed themselves into the countryside. Beginning with their "final offensive" in January 1981, they have demonstrated obvious military abilities. The Salvadorean Armed Forces have been unable to achieve any lasting success in their counterinsurgency operations despite changes of leadership, new strategies, and ongoing material support from the United States. For the guerrillas, a lack of massive support in the major cities of El Salvador and progressively more limited international support have prevented them from going beyond the success of a few spectacular operations. Discouragement and dissensions within guerrilla ranks are not unknown among the guerrillas either, as can be seen in the murder and suicide respectively of two leaders of the FMLN in Managua in 1983.

Kidnappings and terrorist attacks came back in fashion during the 1985 and 1986 while the FDR has lost ground politically on the international front. This is reflected in Duarte's consolidation of power and in a lessening of the guerrillas' offensive capacity. United States aid exceeding $600 million in 1985 has played a key role. Without the Reagan administration's public political support, Duarte's Christian Democratic administration would have had a short life. Economic assistance has proven crucial during the economic crisis and for the military who continually require more training and materiel. This consolidation of power is rather precarious in any case. Duarte does not enjoy the complete support of his military while in the business community he is still regarded as an enemy. Added to these are strikes and union protests during 1985 and 1986 and repeated charges of official corruption.

The struggle is still stalemated. The three forces in conflict do not separately have the strength to triumph. The ruling class, grouped in extreme right parties (ARENA in particular) roundly reject any concessions and intend to turn back the clock. The Christian Democrats and a part of the Armed Forces, with open U.S. support, are attempting to combine "reform and repression" to transform the society while defeating the guerrillas and suppressing all grassroots organizing. The FDR and the FLMN are working towards a much more radical transformation that they are not in a position to carry out. Without a major shift in the balance of power between the forces in conflict, any resolution of this stalemate will depend on an agreement or alliance between two of those forces. Roundtable negotiations between all three forces seem out of the question for the moment.

In Nicaragua, the Sandinistas are attempting to forge a new society. In the five years since Somoza's fall and the revolution's triumph, the great majority of Nicaraguans have experienced successes, threats, and problems. Here, too, the future continues to sow divisiveness.

Reconstruction became the priority the day after Somoza fell. Death and devastation were soon replaced by a recovering economy. In 1980–1981 the indicators were clearly favorable. Production levels had risen to 1977 levels. Overall investments had experienced a jump and the GDP was growing rapidly. Even though the foreign debt was enormous—a legacy mainly from the Somoza period—and terms of trade were not favorable, it seemed that a period of sustained economic growth was not far off. But, an internal political crisis and a showdown with the United States changed the course of events.

From the beginning, the Reagan administration adopted a hard line. In February of 1981, the Sandinistas were labeled as the main arms suppliers to the Salvadorean guerrillas. In April, viewing Nicaragua as a threat to peace in the Isthmus,

Washington suspended all bilateral aid. In December, President Reagan authorized $19 million to finance counterrevolutionary activities in Nicaragua. Military bases in Honduras and joint military maneuvers involving thousands of soldiers and major air and naval forces complete the preventative measures taken against the Nicaraguan threat. There was a truly intimidating noose along the northern border and the coasts of Nicaragua. Direct action was allowed only to the ex-Somoza National Guard forces encamped along the Honduran border along with other groups operating sporadically from Costa Rica. Sabotage and pillaging became a heavy burden on the Nicaraguan economy. In 1982 Managua estimated the toll to be about 8 percent of the total value of exports the year. It rose to about 32 percent of the value of exports the following year. The waste and losses brought about by these sorts of aggression are probably much greater than those from the March and September 1983 offensives, or from even more spectacular events such as the mining of harbors and that attack of fuel depots in October of 1983.

Even if no one can ignore U.S. complicity in these aggressive measures, it would be naive to suppose that they arise exclusively from hostile CIA and Pentagon intentions. They also reflect a deep internal political crisis. The Sandinista program can no longer count on as broad-based a consensus as it enjoyed in 1979 in the first light of the Revolution.

Businessmen withdrew from the Board of National Reconstruction (Junta de Reconstrucción Nacional) in April 1980 after the Sandinista Front modified the compositions of the Council of State (Consejo de Estado), a sort of legislative body. The divisions have widened since then, COSEP (Consejo Superior de la Empresa Privada), or Supreme Council of Private Enterprise, and the Catholic Church hierarchy have not relented in criticizing the regime, accusing it openly of totalitarian tendencies. Political life can hardly be smooth amidst the tensions and external threats that have embroiled Nicaragua since 1982. Consequently, we could understand press censorship, suspension of individual civil rights, and a dramatic increase in political control just as well as natural response by the state to these threats as the emergence of a totalitarian regime.

Political parties play a secondary role in the present confrontation of forces. The Sandinista Front can be described as a grassroots movement organized during the struggle against Somoza and later strengthened by its privileged access to state power. Under these conditions it is hardly surprising that military groups played a primary role and that major bases for the ideology were created only after the revolution. Even though the whole political spectrum, from the most traditional conservatism to the radical left, is displayed through a dozen parties, none of them has sufficient organization, experience, or broad-based impact to attract any attention. After long years of the Somoza family's rule, how could it be otherwise? This relative lack of representativeness of the political parties explains why such organizations as COSEP, the newspaper *La Prensa* (that was itself a focus of opposition to Somoza), or the Church hierarchy are so belligerent. That there are not mediating elements in the conflict also illustrates its character. We are not dealing with an opposition easily managed in an election. There are different economic theories, different concepts of society, and political power clashing. In short, the struggle is one for power not for office.

The ecclesiastical hierarchy's combativeness dramatically demonstrates the lack of a common political framework in the struggle. In its ideological power and organizing ability, the Church is the only institution that can challenge the Sandinista Front in the area of grassroots mobilization. However, that same challenge confronts it with the so-called People's Church, which attempts to embody an "alternative for the poor" within the ideological framework of the Revolution.

International support was very broad in 1979 and 1980, but it too has diminished. There are two reasons. One is the open showdown between Nicaragua and the United States and the U.S. diplomatic efforts to gain support for its Central American policies. However, growing polarization within Nicaragua and especially conflict with the hierarchy of the Catholic Church and the business community have also contributed to the new Nicaragua's international image. Nevertheless, the overwhelming majority of Third World countries continue to look very sympathetically on the regime in Managua in that it is the product of an anti-imperialist and nationalist revolution. The Socialist International also continues supporting the Sandinista government even though several of its member nations have begun to show some dissent.

The greatest support comes from Cuba and the Soviet bloc as well as some Latin American countries. The former have provided technical assistance, direct aid, loans and trade agreements under favorable terms, arms, and military advice. The latter countries, especially Mexico, Venezuela, Colombia, and Panama have offered important diplomatic support that has been epitomized in the deliberations of the Contadora group.

What really is the face of the new Nicaragua? Economically there are two imperatives: (1) to develop new forms of ownership and business practice that would be an alternative to the market economy model; and (2) to guarantee the domestic supply of basic consumer goods. The expropriated possessions of the Somoza family and their coterie ended up as state property classified as "people's property." In 1982 that category amounted to 39 percent of the GDP. We should note, however, that state property, cooperatives, and small production facilities are primary only in the area of retail business and services. Over half of the land and cattle sector and the manufacturing industry is in the hands of large and midsized private enterprises. Consequently from a structural point of view, we can speak of a mixed economy. The current crisis situation, especially the growing confrontations of the state with COSEP, have led to a dramatic decline in private investment. But the regime is trying to offer guarantees to private ownership, primarily in the land and cattle sector. In

December 1983 a decree guaranteed that no agricultural lands would be expropriated regardless of size provided they were productive. The government exercises a strict control over exports and promotes participation by workers in various levels of decision making. Up to now the Nicaraguan economy has followed the path of a market economy. Planning, as it is practiced in Soviet bloc countries, is barely in its infancy at best. Economic warfare and enormous expenses for defense explain the increasing difficulties in supplying sufficient foodstuffs and basic goods. Yet there is also speculation and hoarding by businesses as well as the government's own inability to find a solution to the problem of how to achieve equitable distribution.

Literacy campaigns and improvements in public health delivery can be counted as successes of the regime. They have contributed as much to the improvement in the quality of life as to consciousness raising and grassroots organizing and have politically benefited the Sandinista Front. Open unemployment and underemployment in informal sector service activities are still widespread and are serious social problems whose solution is yet to be found. Education, broad-based participation in decision making, and well-being are not easily achieved in a backward underdeveloped country such as Nicaragua. This is especially so when trying to build a future in the middle of a civil war and international aggression.

There are three main ideological sources for the Sandinista Revolution. First is the historical *Sandinismo*. This derives from Sandino's struggles against the U.S. invasion during 1927–1933. Its political thought is nationalist and anti-imperialist and it blends into the almost mythological folk hero of Sandino himself. Second is what we might call a Third World socialism represented quintessentially by the Cuban experience, but also derived from some African and Asian revolutions. Third is the Christianity of the "People's Church" that is founded upon what has come to be known as liberation theology. The symbiosis of these three ideological sources has been facilitated by the virtual absence of charismatic leadership within the Sandinista Front. The blending of these varied elements has also promoted a broad-based allegiance with its message deeply rooted in cultural traditions. Heroes and martyrs populate the new collective memory of the past. A new national identity is coming into being.

Will the development of a participatory democracy be possible? It is not easy to give a straightforward answer to this crucial question. There are bureaucratic and authoritarian tendencies at the heart of the regime itself that cannot be ignored. The close identification of the Sandinista Front with the state, the fundamental role of the Army and its command structure, reinforced by urgent defense needs, all further these tendencies just as does the increasingly influential Cuban model. Then there are serious doubts about the realistic chances of creating a participatory democracy when, as in Nicaragua, there is historically a lack of actual experience with representative democracy.

The opposition forces are not united. Sandinistas who have recanted have been unable to offer an alternative between the present regime and a return to a Somoza-style rule. The Somozistas lead the guerrilla war in the north and along the Honduran border. After the November 1984 elections, the chances of achieving peace seem more remote than ever. The foreseeable triumph of the Sandinista Front consolidated the regime's continuity but it has not increased its legitimacy. Defense needs, on the other hand, have led to forced conscription of recruits and to the formation of a rather strong defense force.

During 1985 and 1986 the Reagan Administration considerably increased pressure on Nicaragua through an economic boycott and significant military and financial assistance to the Contras. Internally, the Sandinista regime has hardened. The newspaper *La Prensa* was shut down in June 1986 and run-ins with the Catholic Church hierarchy have increased. The economic weight of the war as well as an unforeseen drought have brought new hardships. The numbers of peasants along the Honduran-Nicaraguan border displaced by the conflict now number possibly as many as 250,000. The new Constitution, ratified in November 1986, reaffirms the basic principles articulated in 1979: political pluralism, mixed economy, nonalignment. Nicaragua's future, nevertheless, rests more than ever on the chances of all sides coming together.

Geography once again controls the future of Honduras. Once more, as during the latter half of the nineteenth century and the beginning of the twentieth, we are dealing with a pivotal region that is strategically decisive for what is happening in Guatemala, El Salvador, and Nicaragua.

The change began to occur in 1980. Pentagon strategists quickly attained important concessions with little political cost. This is how U.S. bases were set up, the Honduran Army was reequipped and impressive military maneuvers were carried out. The 1981 elections that ended nine years of military rule added a certain legitimacy to an already compromised situation. Still, real power remained with the chief of the Armed Forces rather than with the elected president. Between January 1982 and March 1984, General Gustavo Álvarez Martínez ruled with an iron hand, closely imitating his Guatemalan and Salvadorean counterparts. As a loyal ally of Washington, he signed military accords behind the back of elected officials and seriously jeopardized the integrity of legislative authority. He unswervingly supported Somoza's former National Guardsmen who were encamped along the Honduran-Nicaraguan border, and fiercely pursued Salvadorean refugees. State terrorism also surfaced: illegal detentions, torture, and disappearances bedeviled Honduran politics during those unfortunate years.

Álvarez Martínez's fall, in March 1984, was an event of great importance. It implied the military's most repressive elements had retreated, although perhaps only temporarily. The 1985 national elections and the political environment in which they took place—open courting of vested interests (clientelismo) based on personal appeal (personalismo)—reveal how fragile the political system continues to be. Under these conditions, the political power wielded by the military continues to be as great as before, perhaps even growing.

In the last five years of crisis, Costa Rica is still an island of calm in the storm. This is not because Costa Rica has remained unaffected by economic upsets. There has been, rather, a surprising degree of political stability, a minimum of controversy in public opinion, and a widespread confidence in the capacity of the country's political system to respond to the difficult challenges.

Relations with Managua have been, by contrast, much more fraught with problems. Most of the Nicaraguan opposition not linked to Somoza has taken refuge in Costa Rica and enjoys a broad sympathy. The mass media constantly harp on the alleged dangers inherent in Sandinismo, and there is no lack of border incidents with Nicaragua. Costa Rican diplomacy has revealed, however, some subtleties vis-à-vis its traditional alignment with U.S. diplomacy. Costa Rica, Honduras, and El Salvador together joined to form the Central American Democratic Community (Comunidad Democrática Centroamericana). This was an unsuccessful effort in 1982 to isolate Nicaragua. However, Monge's declaration of neutrality in November 1983 clearly expressed the intent not to involve Costa Rica in the various regional conflicts. The peace issue was uppermost in the political contest leading up to the presidential elections of 1986. This issue provided the president-elect, Oscar Arias Sánchez, with an important mandate.

The economic crisis has worsened the living conditions of the majority of Costa Ricans. Housing and access to land—in certain areas of the country—seem to be particularly urgent needs. Health, education, and employment, by contrast, have been less impacted. The cost of providing for those needs has been a continuing deficit in the treasury and has entailed postponing very drastic fiscal measures such as those recommending adherence to revenues or the requirements of international finance institutions. But this cost seems minimal if one considers that it has maintained social peace. A modicum of economic stability since 1984 has come about mainly due to U.S. economic aid, which has flowed in a relatively generous fashion.

How can the major achievements in social and political development be maintained where the economy shows serious signs of structural weaknesses that will demand considerable adjustments in the more or less immediate future? This is Costa Rica's challenge over the next few years.

## AN UNCERTAIN FUTURE

Insecurity about the future is perhaps the best index to the depth and repercussions of the crisis in Central America.

The economic alternatives are unclear for countries that are as poor, so terribly dependent on world markets and beset by innumerable structural problems. Fragmentation and a diversity of political ideologies also make it difficult to present a common front to the developed countries and entail putting on hold rebuilding the Central American Common Market (Mercado Común Centroamericano). Taking advantage of new (and rare) strategies to link up with world markets will probably reinforce this same fragmentation of vested interests and ideologies.

The direction of U.S. policy will define many situations in the near future. It may well mean a major increase in military involvement in the Isthmus. The parameters of confrontation are naturally unpredictable just as is its outcome. It is a chess game with too many pieces and too many players. Honduras is an excellent example of walking a tightrope. The former Somoza guardsmen and the FDN (National Democratic Front) troops that operate inside Honduras along the border are a major military force. Even though its offensive ability closely depends on CIA aid, it is naive to deny that for the Honduran government this military presence constitutes a sort of parallel state. The role of U.S. forces acquires thereby a much broader scope than being merely a "guarantee" against eventual Nicaraguan aggression. All this once again indicates that in war there are no innocents.

The political future is equally cloudy. 1984 and 1985 were election years. But it would be naive to imagine that elections in Guatemala, El Salvador, Nicaragua, and Honduras signal a dramatic step forward in democracy. Violence and exclusion from participation for some groups have limited the freedom to choose electorally. International pressures have likewise affected the electoral processes themselves. We would be naive utopians to imagine that reforms imposed from above or a successful revolution can give rise immediately to a freer and more democratic society. The electoral process and political participation require a prior historical experience that cannot be avoided. Democracy has never emerged from suffering and desperation.

The effort to bring peace to the region seems to have picked up new life in 1987. The 1986 Contadora initiative and plan was not signed. During that year the chances of general or limited agreements seemed more remote than ever. In 1987, however, everything suddenly changed. On August 7, the Central American presidents subscribed to the preliminary peace accords proposed by Dr. Oscar Arias Sán-chez, president of Costa Rica. These accords also included the following features: amnesty, a cease fire, prohibition of the use of territory as a base for armed aggression against a neighbor, democratization, and an end of aid to rebels. The accords contained a schedule of dates for future steps and mechanisms for initiating concrete actions in each of the basic areas covered by the accords. Since the Salvadorean guerrilla conflict had by then lost much of its offensive initiative and was far from any chance of victory, the Nicaraguan Contras were the only real losers in these accords. Similarly, the Sandinista regime viewed its legitimacy reinforced by the accords.

How was such an apparently drastic turnaround possible in such a short time? The first reason is, evidently, the U.S. foreign policy crisis arising out of the Iran-Contra affair toward the end of 1986. The second reason arises from developments in Central American politics. In Nicaragua, the Contras failed to incite a general uprising while at the same time the country was in the throes of a major economic crisis. In El Salvador, the guerrilla offensive was subsiding while concurrently the Duarte government was consolidating its power relative to the guerrillas. Honduras was not concealing its growing uneasiness with the irregular Contra forces camped along the border with Nicaragua while, at the same time, the presidents of Guatemala and Costa Rica chose to pursue realistic regional policies with a sincere desire to achieve peace in the area. We may also now be seeing, at the bottom of it all, a general weariness that is understandable after almost ten years of civil strife, economic crises, and widespread violence. We should not overlook the fact that in the latter half of 1987 political initiative had returned to Central American hands. In this context, we need to consider the notable originality, tenacity, and courage of the Costa Rican president whose efforts were rewarded with the Nobel Peace Prize in 1987.

None of us can know whether at this point we are witnessing the opening of a pathway toward a lasting peace or merely an interlude full of hopefulness after which war and violence will once again return. We can highlight what conditions are most necessary to consolidate these gains. In the short run, there needs to be created a margin of confidence for negotiation between the principal combatants: the guerrillas and the Salvadorean government, the Contras and the Sandinista government. After this, there is the crucial issue of how much each of the sides is willing to concede in negotiations or, in other terms, how much can be concretely gained through each side's concessions. In the middle and long run, matters are more precarious. Democratization, social progress on a regional scale, and the chances for real concrete reforms depend heavily on economic reconstruction and the condition of the world economy. All of these in turn hinge on the possibility of ending the process of the "impoverishing growth" of the past. Whether or not all of this comes to pass will also depend on the dynamics of the social forces in play as well as what we might call the ability of the major players to learn from experience.

If there is any positive side of the crisis of violence during the past few years it is that the combatants will have learned the real limits to their ambitions. Transgressing those limits makes coexistence impossible. In essence, peace is lasting only if it is based on strategies of social coexistence that are more equitable for everyone.

# Epilogue
# The Sentence of History

## THE BORDERS OF THE PAST

The failures of the ruling classes have always changed the course of history. This is undeniably what is happening in part today in Central America. With the exception of Costa Rica, landowners and business people were unable to transform the agrarian capitalism instituted at the close of the nineteenth century. Progress was crushed by the great wheel of misery. The great majority of the underclass were bereft of dignity. An Indian was still valued as less than a horse. It matters little whether we refer to the ruling class as bourgeoisie, oligarchy, or aristocracy. The fact is that they did not succeed in forging a new collaboration and consensus to replace the crumbling colonial paternalism. Control rested therefore exclusively on exploitation, violence, and terror.

Premature shortsightedness? Uncontrolled greed? Perhaps both. Responses to the inevitable erosion of power in a changing world obey in any case the same design. At the end of his magnificent study on the crisis of the English aristocracy in the seventeeth century, Lawrence Stone remarks that when the nobility saw their privileges threatened they only thought to react with "overweening arrogance" which was an unmistakable sign of "fundamental insecurity." By analogy, we can make the same observation here. The English peers, however, attempted to justify their privileges with evidence from history: noble ancestry, rights enshrined in tradition, and folk memory. The Central American bourgeoisie, when confronted, never had such scruples or rational demeanor. Their anti-Communist hysteria was an adequate defense and moral justification to reject any genuine grassroots demands or claims for justice.

Being unable to achieve social change is not synonymous with economic failure. Far from it: growth in the nineteeth century had some spectacular aspects, one proof being the accumulation of personal fortunes. The profitability of businesses and use of modern technology are likewise not at issue. Rather, it is economic efficiency without correspondingly suitable social relations, or growth without distribution. There have clearly been structural traits that underlie this, but a lack of political will or the cultural precariousness of the ruling elite are also as important.

By studying the case of Costa Rica we can get a feel for possibilities and limitations. While traveling through the Isthmus in the 1940s, William Krehm, a writer for *Time* magazine, considered that here was a "lucky accident of nature," a sort of "Shrangri-La," this in a region abounding in dictators and corrupt military. When he ended his interview with president Teodoro Picado, he had the feeling he had been conversing with a rural doctor in his cozy office. He was even more astonished when he talked with Monsignor Sanabria, the archbishop of Costa Rica whom the rightist press labeled a "communist." If William Krehm were to retrace his journey today, forty years later, his astonishment would not cease. Infant mortality has declined to about nineteen per thousand. The life expectancy is one of Latin America's highest. The degree of control over infectious diseases exceeds all expectations. The electoral process and political life is comparable to the United States or Western Europe. All this is true of an underdeveloped country that finds itself in the middle of a deep economic crisis and which shares in no small measure the misfortunes of the whole region. The great value of comparing this unique experience can be summarized by two main observations. First, it shows that democracy and social reform is possible in Central America regardless of any "curse" of the culture, racial defect, or any sort of "evil heritage" of Spanish colonialism. There are arguments that few take seriously but are all too often repeated. Second, it demonstrates the limits on how much one country's historical experience can apply to another's. Reform and democracy are the products of a long historical development combining chance and necessity, individual will and collective struggle. Reforms can be quickly imitated or even be forceably imposed. There are certain instances of "revolution from above." But, it would be illusory to suppose similar political outcomes in all societies. Democracy always emerges out of a long collective experience that entails not only certain feedoms but also a certain political culture and education. Opportunity, by contrast, sets harsh limits to the ability to reform. Even if the "right time" might be just empty words in the mouths of politicians, their historical significance is often crucial. Simple changes, often insignificant, have sometimes managed to prevent everything from falling apart, whereas radical reforms at the wrong moment frequently have been a hollow solution to placate social strife.

Both success and failure in involving the masses are well illustrated in the following example. In August 1934 the Atlantic Coast banana plantations in Costa Rica were shaken by a major strike. The leaders of the recently founded Communist Party of Costa Rica displayed their outstanding organizing skills and within a few days over 10,000 workers were on strike. Towards month's end, the government intervened and worked out an agreement with the strikers. The United Fruit Company did not participate in the negotiations and it soon became quite clear that the Company had no intentions of fulfilling the agreement that had been reached. The strike broke out again in September. There were some signs of violence and the police jailed the Communist leaders of the strike movement. However, shortly afterwards, during negotiations for a new contract with the banana company, the government ratified in law most of what the strikers had been demanding.

Costa Rican president Ricardo Jiménez, a pragmatic Liberal of the old school, recognized the justice of the strikers' demands. In an interview at the end of August 1934, he noted that the Communists behaved legally, but commented that ideas could not as successfully be opposed by force as by other ideas. If the Communist leaders actually represented the majority of the workers, then it would be necessary to deal with them just as had happened in the United States, England, and France. As a justice-loving citizen, he could not deny hearing what was just and reasonable in what those humble laborers were protesting about. The president observed that laws needed to change along with the times. He argued that the right to strike was protected by law in Mexico. During Porfirio Díaz's government, however, official forces broke strikes and attacked the workers. This was exactly what some in Costa Rica were asking for in their fears about what was taking place on the Atlantic Coast.

In his confidential communications, the U.S. military attaché to Costa Rica viewed president Jiménez as a liberal who rather resembled President Roosevelt in his thinking. But the attaché was concerned that his liberal attitude might unleash a wave of strikes and labor strife throughout the entire country. The United Fruit Company did everything it could to resist the strikers' demands. Possibly the most constructive outcome of the strike was the institutionalization of the union's struggle. In accepting the strikers' demands as legitimate and just, Ricardo Jiménez clearly saw that this did not entail an overall commitment to Communist Party ideology. Rather, correcting certain injustices within the system itself would prevent even greater problems.

By the end of 1931, political upheaval in El Salvador took a very serious turn. The military coup of December 2 elevated the war minister, General Maximiliano Hernández Martínez to power as chief of state. The ravages of the economic crisis were worsening and social unrest was constantly boiling. The situation was particularly critical on the coffee plantations that were located in the parts of the country most densely populated by Indians. The newly founded Salvadorean Communist Party was intensely involved in politics and union organizing.

Social distress and repression were evident the whole year under the constitutionally elected government of president Arturo Araujo. After the coup, matters worsened rapidly. Attempted strikes became numerous as did clashes with the forces of repression. Social unrest skyrocketed. The Communist Party did participate, however, in the municipal and legislative elections on January 3–5 and 10–12 in 1932. The incidence of fraud was so flagrant that even the rightist parties protested. With the write-in candidates and public voting, it was not hard to identify Communist leaders and sympathizers. In light of the electoral farce, imminent strikes, labor unrest, and the threat of repression, Communist leaders endeavored to formally talk with President Hernández Martínez. They were carrying a simple platform to him: improve working conditions, raise salaries, allow right of unionization in the rural areas. The leaders seemed to realize that they would not otherwise be able to prevent the spontaneous outburst of popular wrath. The meeting was actually with the war minister, since the president feigned illness with a toothache. There were no results. What happened next is quite well known and had the inevitability of a Greek tragedy. The Communist leaders knew that with or without an uprising they would be repressed, and they knew they could not contain the workers' boiling discontent. They decided to work for an insurrection on January 16, 1932. In the meantime, the police rounded up the leaders, but the insurrection finally took place on January 22 in the countryside. Shortly beforehand, a subversive plot failed in the (police) barracks in San Salvador. In the end, hundreds of peasants armed with machetes, sticks, and stones faced government troops. The capital of San Salvador was seized with fear, but the situation was quickly brought under control. Some 10,000 to 30,000 were victims of detentions and executions. A U.S. diplomat noted:

> a remarkable feature of the armed attacks on the communists was the coolness and courage with [which] the poor Indians who could not possibly have given any coherent idea of what communism really is, met their death. Photographs which

have arrived in the capital show them before firing squads with quizzical, almost amused expressions on their faces. In innumerable cases, people were executed not because there was any evidence of their communism but rather because they told the Government forces that they were communists.[1]

The chain of events could not be clearer: (1) a union struggle that got nowhere; (2) an electoral campaign mocked by fraud and crackdowns; (3) efforts to negotiate with the government that were similarly fruitless; (4) insurrection; (5) bloody repression; and (6) the trauma of terror and forty years of silent infamy against the peasants. The path had two consequences. On the one hand, there was a premeditated refusal to include the lower classes. On the other, the ruling class was no longer able to distinguish between claims for redress and revolutionary uprisings. In the long run, this blindness ends up being a factor of progressive weakness.

This ruling class behavior defines a pattern of evolution which will have a decisive effect on the future of Central American societies. It may be that the current situation in Costa Rica and Nicaragua is a mirror reflecting a possible future of the other countries, which is gradual transformation blending social reform and democracy. The alternative is a revolutionary solution that will lead to some sort of Third World socialism. It does not seem very likely that Guatemala, Honduras, and El Salvador can easily take this first path. One might argue for the possibility of a middle road or of a very slow evolution, but one that leads to a political and social structure similar to Costa Rica's. The latter is perhaps more likely for Honduras, but it is not impossible for the other countries. We ought to state that historical experience reveals, as much for Guatemala as for El Salvador, the failure of this middle road. The fall of Arbenz in 1954 and the quick suffocation of Colonel Julio Rivera's timid reforms in El Salvador between 1961 and 1967 both illustrate this failure quite eloquently.

## U.S. INFLUENCE

We do not need to further emphasize the enormous importance of international factors, especially U.S. influence, in

Central America's destiny. After 1979, everything took on a new dimension. The region's conflicts have not only stirred up public opinion deeply both in the United States and Europe but real or imagined threats—it does not matter which—have transformed the region into an essential element of U.S. foreign policy. What we are dealing with, in other words, is a serious crisis of U.S. influence in an area very important strategically but traditionally forgotten and despised.

This unpredictability derives not only from which party happens to occupy the White House or the impact of the personality of foreign policy makers. It also arises from complexities in how the different vested interests affected will link up. We may perhaps suggest some general guidelines about that foreign policy. The course that U.S. foreign policy will take is impossible to foresee but some generalities can be mentioned. First, strategic interests and the manner in which they are regarded have a major impact on any critical decision. Second, policy dealing with issues of security or matters of worldwide interest has never been defined as something exclusively pragmatic or applying just locally to a particular region. George F. Kennan observed astutely that there has always existed a sort of "congenital aversion of Americans to taking specific decisions on specific problems," which is reflected in a "persistent urge to seek universal formulae or doctrine in which to clothe and justify particular actions."[2] Overthrowing Arbenz in 1954 or eliminating the present Sandinista regime are justified as necessary to contain communism and the imagined Soviet meddling in the region. They are translated into mere episodes in a larger heroic struggle between the Good Guys and the Bad Guys. Third, placing such localized problems as are Central America's into a global East-West context also affects relations between the United States and its allies. A source of conflict, much larger than anticipated, has been efforts to convince some European or Latin American countries about the legitimacy of Washington's policy positions. The world today is much less polarized than it was in the 1950s. The diversity of interests and ambitions tempers simplifications. Fourth, after the Vietnam War and the Watergate events, moral scruples have grown in broad sectors of public opinion and among U.S. policymakers. This greatly complicates any decision about direct military intervention which has the risk of becoming another prolonged adventure.

If we peruse U.S.–Latin American relations over the last ten to fifteen years, we will see some new trends. A new nationalism is visible with some signs of Latin American solidarity and a clear tendency to present a common front toward the United States. Witness the renegotiation of the Panama Canal Treaty in 1976–1977, the fall of Somoza in 1979, the Malvinas War [Falklands War] in 1982. Under these conditions, it seems unlikely there will be a return to the past. It may be that we see being defined a "new accord" the basis of a new order in U.S.–Latin America relations. Even though only the future will reveal what the eventual outcome will be, we can assert confidently that in this redefinition of old and bitter relations, Latin America will have a more independent and active role than before. It is hard to deny that what happens in Central America will decisively affect the mutual advantages visible in the outline of that new order.

## THE QUESTION OF NATIONAL IDENTITY

All our searching questions about the future have deep roots in the past. Some questions acquire a greater urgency from a historical perspective. The economic and political viability of a fragmented Central America is one of them. Since the crisis of the Central American Federation in the first half of the nineteenth century up to the disintegration of the Common Market in the latter half of the twentieth, the utopia of a union has been tirelessly repeated. The near future does not give us much hope. The theme of unity—perhaps more realistically that of solidarity between the countries—will resurface. There is more than one reason. The size of the countries, economically speaking, requires that they integrate. Their small size, politically, presents security issues that are virtually nonexistent for larger countries. How some countries will fare in the future will vitally affect rather quickly the fortunes of their neighbors.

The fact that the issue of unity keeps resurfacing for various reasons also means that, to an extent, the national identities of the various Central American countries are not yet quite solidified. A good indication of this situation is the relevance of the Indian question in Guatemala. Here we could be dealing with the most agonizing and traumatic legacy of the past.

Just one example, out of many, will illustrate more graphically than any generalization or theoretical analysis, the degree of the Indians' brutal and remorseless subjection. Albertina Saravia Enríquez presents our example with passion in a moving book. The event deals with the crime of Julián Tzul that happened in a village in the Guatemalan highlands in November 1963.

The local police chief bound over the prisoner Tzul to the Lower Court (Tribunal de la Primera Instancia) with the following report:

> Yesterday at three in the afternoon, I, as chief of police, and two of my officers, after learning who had murdered the elderly Juan Ajpop Tacam, established that Julián Tzul Tajivoy, on the seventh of November, at three in the morning, attacked with a club the sorcerer when the latter was involved in carrying out acts of sorcery against the assailant, for which motive Tzul struck him several times about the head and other parts of his body, afterwards leaving him seated on a rock. Later he went to his home, then leaving he went to the residence of his neighbor Mariano Ixcaquic Tzul to inform him that he had just killed the sorcerer and to ask what he could do. To this Ixcaquic advised him to leave the victim where he was, that he burn the club and that he had committed the act because Mr. Juan was harming him. Julián Tzul Tajivoy voluntarily confessed to all of this after being questioned by me, as chief of police, in charge of the precinct station.

In the course of the trial, the defense managed to establish the following facts: (1) Julián Tzul was known to be an honorable person and of good conduct; (2) Juan Ajpop Tacam was widely known to be a "sorcerer;" (3) the village believed that the sudden death of Julián Tzul's wife had been brought about by sorcery; (4) the place where the crime occurred was a shrine were sorcery was regularly practiced. The defense also brought forth the opinions of two expert anthropologists who offered in generous detail testimony on the beliefs and customs of the Indians in that area. Their testimony established not only the panic that sorcery engenders among the Indians but also the Indians' belief in the power of prayers given before altars or in such shrines.

In brief, the defense argued that for cultural reasons the murderous behavior of Julián Tzul had occurred in a situation of "overwhelming fear," which circumstance removed his culpability. The attorney for the defense spoke as follows in one part of his summary:

> Written and published laws depend on literate Guatemalans to [be able to] read them. How many literate citizens has the Republic?
>
> The duty you have, your Honor, is to judge a fellow Guatemalan citizen. A Guatemalan who lives, thinks, reasons, loves, reacts, and seeks enjoyment in a world totally different and alien to our own. He lives and moves to standards of behavior based on other values; he employs other remedies to satisfy injury; he has a different understanding of authority and law from our own; he spends his life obeying laws of custom not written laws because he cannot read; he is governed by another social structure.
>
> It is well-known and obvious that the Indians of Guatemala live in greater backwardness than do we *Ladinos*.[3]

The prosecution was represented by a prosecutor from the Attorney General (Ministerio Público) and asked to have the homicide considered willful and for a sentence of twenty years in prison. He argued against the notion of "overwhelming fear" and that the views of the expert witnesses were very general, inapplicable to the case at issue. Besides, he declared:

> The position of the expert witnesses, regarding the "over-

whelming fear" that engendered the enormous crime we are considering, contradicts reality since, if we allow that those who know that they are the victims of sorcery can suffer some fear, this fear cannot become overwhelming and lead to bloody acts.

Were this the case every day we would have within our Indian communities numberless violent acts, bodily injury and murders, but this does not happen.

If the statistics on this sort of homicide were studied with respect to the motives, other causes such as alcohol, sex, land ownership, etc., appear in almost all instances, the element of evil sorcery being incidental.

The Tribunal sentenced Julián Tzul to ten years in prison but excused him from paying court costs because of his "obvious indigency." This sentence was subsequently upheld by the Supreme Court. Julián Tzul's exclamation upon hearing the sentence gave Albertina Saravia her title: "The *Ladino* screwed me."

For the mass of the backward, oppressed, and exploited peasants, the Nation is something whose invention has yet to be completed.

## BUILDING A FUTURE

To win a future of peace and dignity is the principal ambition of the great majority of Central Americans. Regrettably, to achieve this goal will probably entail sacrificing further thousands of lives. We need to recognize that these multitudes are weighted down not by years but by centuries of backwardness and humiliations. Fray Las Casas wrote over four centuries ago about the gruesome genocide of the indigenous civilizations. Lands with "great numbers" of people, "admirable fruit groves," orchards and farms were all wiped out by "such slaughters, cruelties, so many captivities and injustices that the human tongue is powerless to express them." For some he exaggerated, for others he was accurate, but he offered thousands of pages of denunciation, indictment of the exploitation, and struggle without quarter for human dignity. Unfortunately, that incriminating testimony has found its match in recent history: in the tortures, repression, and slaughters that have been unleashed upon the peasants and workers, common people whose only ambition is to live with hope and dignity.

Imprisonment and torture have never been absent in the Isthmus's history. But we have to go back over four centuries to the tragic period of the Conquest to find like numbers of death, such woe in body and soul. There is probably no more ghastly feature than the sacrifice of innocent children. Let us hear from a witness to the massacre carried out by the Salvadorean Army in La Joya on December 10, 1981:

> And the children there, in La Joya, crying and screaming for their mothers and they were all grabbed, kicked and beaten, and then they killed them, some by slitting their throats, others were set on fire still alive, and one soldier almost went mad because a child wouldn't die, first he stabbed him and the boy didn't die, then he threw gasoline on him and the boy still didn't die, then when he saw the child wasn't going to die, he machine-gunned him and then the boy died . . .

Their brutalization is such that the soldiers do not even know why they are killing. The peasants, for their part, cannot understand why they are being slaughtered. In his peculiar Spanish, this is also what a Guatemalan Indian is saying. He is a survivor of the massacre committed by the army at the San Francisco (Huehuetenango) ranch on July 17, 1982:

> This is how I came, Father . . . I'm just listening again, but with sorrow,' cause in my heart I'm with the dead. Because I've surely seen, I'm looking at the killing of my brothers, everybody, buddies, everybody. We are all of us like brothers. That's why my heart is crying all the time . . . They don't say, "This is the crime, this is the evidence." Nobody did that. To know that it happens. Nobody's pointing nothing out. "This is the crime, here's another." Nobody's saying. They just kill. That's all.

No one knows if the aftermath of such iniquity and shame will include a better future. Fray Las Casas certainly believed so in the sixteenth century and did not withhold his efforts.

Monsignor Oscar Arnulfo Romero, the archbishop of San Salvador murdered on March 24, 1980, spoke these words in a sermon delivered shortly before his death:

> I am certain that all the blood that has been spilled and all the pain of the families of so many victims will not be in vain . . . This blood and pain will sow new and ever greater numbers of seeds in Salvadoreans who will become conscious of the responsibility they have to build a more just and humane society . . .

The days go by. The rains return in May each year. Peasants once again plant corn and in their way push life into the heart of the earth. The future may be inscrutable; the sentence of the past is still with us. But we can no longer believe they deserve yet another stillborn Spring.

# Chronology

1502  Columbus explores the coasts of Honduras, Nicaragua, Costa Rica, and Panama.

1513  Balboa crosses the Panama Isthmus and discovers the Southern Sea (Pacific Ocean).

1519  Panama City founded. Gulf of Dulce and Nicoya Gulf discovered. Mexico conquered.

1524  Pedro de Alvarado founds Santiago de los Caballeros in Guatemala. Hernández de Córdoba founds cities of León and Granada.

1525  Cities of Trujillo (Honduras) and San Salvador (El Salvador) founded.

1531–1532  The bishopric of León built. Fray Las Casas arrives in Nicaragua.

1534  The bishopric of Guatemala built.

1536–1540  Indian slaves exported from Nicaragua to Peru.

1537  City of Comayagua [Honduras] founded. First bishop of Guatemala consecrated.

1540–1575  Surge in cocoa production in Izalco (El Salvador).

1542  The Court on Boundaries created.

1548–1550  The Court on Boundaries moved to Guatemala.

1552  City of Sonsonate [El Salvador] founded.

1561  Juan de Cavallón penetrates the Central Valley of Costa Rica.

1563  The Court on Boundaries moved to Panama.

1564  City of Cartago (Costa Rica) founded.

1570  The Court on Boundaries reopened in Guatemala. Throughout the entire colonial period its jurisdiction remained from Chiapas to Costa Rica.

1579    The settlement of Real de Minas founded by inhabitants from Tegucigalpa.

1582    The Jesuits arrive.

1589    Pirates settle Blufields.

1590–1620    The first surge in indigo production.

1597    City of Portobelo founded; city of Nombre de Dios abandoned [Panama].

1604–1612    Fray Verdelete attempts conversion to Christianity in Mosquitia.

1605    The Port of Santo Tomás de Castilla on the north coast of Guatemala completed.

1631–1633    The English found settlements on Providencia Island and Cape Gracias a Dios.

1639–1640    Pirate attacks along the north coast of Honduras.

1643    The Dutch sack the port city of Trujillo [Honduras]. The Spanish abandon this port until 1789.

1655    The English take Jamaica.

1660    The first printing press established in Guatemala.

1662    First English settlement in Belize.

1665    Pirate attacks on cities of Granada, León, and Realejo [Nicaragua].

1681    The University of San Carlos (Guatemala) inaugurated.

1684–1686    Pirate attacks worsen along the coasts of Costa Rica and Nicaragua.

1699    The English establish themselves in Río Tinto (Honduras).

1700    The Bourbons assume the Spanish Throne. War of Succession; Peace of Utrecht in 1713.

1704–1709    Attacks by zambos-mosquitos in Nicaragua and Costa Rica.

1729    First issue of *Gaceta de Guatemala* (Guatemala Gazette) appears.

1731    The Mint of Guatemala created.

1739    The War of Jenkins' Ear. English attack all along the Central American coasts. City of Portobelo [Panama] destroyed.

1742    Archbishopric of Guatemala founded.

1752–1775    Fort Omoa [Honduras] built.

1763    Treaty of Paris; England agrees to destroy its fortifications along the Atlantic Coast of Central America, but will retain rights to lumber.

1767    Jesuits expelled.

1770–1800    Major surge in indigo production in El Salvador.

1773    Earthquakes in Guatemala. Capital city destroyed; it is moved to present location 1775–1776.

1778    Fort Omoa [Honduras] and Fort Santo Tomás opened to intercolonial trade.

1779–1783    War between England and Spain. Captain General Matías de Gálvez frustrates English efforts to invade Nicaragua, but does not succeed in dislodging them from Belize and Mosquitía.

1785–1786    The Intendencies of San Salvador, Chiapas, Honduras, and León [Nicaragua] established.

1793    Administrative Office for the Resolution of Commercial Disputes (*Consulado*) of Guatemala created.

1797–1799    Trade is authorized with neutral states which especially favors U.S. ships. English smuggling spreads along the entire Atlantic Coast.

1808    France invades Spain. Guatemala supports Ferdinand VII.

1811–1814    Independence movements in San Salvador, León, Granada [Nicaragua], and Belén (Guatemala).

1812    Constitution of Cádiz enacted [Spain].

1814–1818    Absolutist reaction [Spain].

1821    Independence and annexation for Mexico.

1823    Annexation of Mexico fails. Complete Independence declared on July 1.

1824    Federal Republic organized. Nicoya annexed to Costa Rica.

1825    Arce is first President of the Federation.

1826–1829    Civil war.

1829–1830    Printing presses established in Honduras, Costa Rica, and Nicaragua.

1830–1839    Morazán is president of Central American Federation.

1831–1838    Mariano Gálvez governs in Guatemala. Liberal reforms carried out.

1837–1840    Cholera epidemic. Indian uprising led by Rafael Carrera, in Guatemala.

1838–1839    Federal Republic disintegrates.

1839–1865    Carrera governs or controls political life in Guatemala.

1839–1850    Continual English threat; they occupy islands of Bahía, San Juan del Norte, and Tigre in the Gulf of Fonseca.

1840    Carrera defeats Morazán.

1840    Slow consolidation of coffee exporting in Costa Rica.

1842    Convention of Chinandega (Confederation Pact signed by Honduras, Nicaragua, and El Salvador).

1843    English establish a protectorate over Mosquitia.

1847–1848    Central American Nations declare themselves sovereign and independent.

1850    Clayton-Bulwer Treaty on interoceanic shipping between England and the United States.

1855–1867    Walker arrives in Nicaragua. "National War" and the Filibusters expelled.

1859    Guatemala recognizes English sovereignty over Belize in exchange for a road connecting Guatemala City with the Atlantic Coast.

1860    Coffee growing expands in Guatemala and El Salvador.

1870–1876    Liberal reforms in Costa Rica, Guatemala, Honduras, and El Salvador.

1885    Central American unification movement of Justo Rufino Barrios. Barrios dies in Battle of Chalchuapa.

1889–1902    Liberal democracy consolidated in Costa Rica.

1893    Liberal revolution in Nicaragua. Regime of José Santos Zelaya (1893–1909).

1894    Zelaya occupies Mosquitia.

1898–1920    Estrada Cabrera rules Guatemala.

1899 United Fruit Company established. Rise of the banana companies (1900–1929).

1901 Hay–Pauncefote Treaty. England releases the United States from the Clayton–Bulwer Treaty obligations.

1903 Panama's Independence; Canal Treaty.

1907 Washington conferences.

1912–1933 U.S. occupy Nicaragua.

1914 Panama Canal inaugurated.

1916 Bryan–Chamorro Treaty.

1920s Worker unionization flourishes. Communist Parties formed in Guatemala, Honduras, El Salvador, and Costa Rica.

1923 Washington Accords.

1927–1934 Sandino's uprising in Nicaragua.

1930–1945 Strong repercussions from the world economic crisis; World War II has negative impact from the closing of European export markets.

1931–1944 Dictatorships of Ubico and Hernández Martínez in Guatemala and El Salvador respectively.

1932 Peasant uprising in El Salvador.

1933–1948 Dictatorship of Carías in Honduras.

1934 Great banana strike in Costa Rica.

1937–1978 Somoza dynasty in Nicaragua.

1940 Washington Agreements: Quotas set up for coffee exports.

1944–1954 Reforms in Guatemala during the governments of Arévalo and Arbenz.

1947–1958 Very significant rise in coffee prices.

1948 Civil War in Costa Rica. Figueres triumphs along with Social Democrats. Strong support for reformist path.

1954 CIA intervenes and Arbenz falls from power in Guatemala. Major banana workers strike in Honduras.

1957–1957 Villeda Morales reformist regime in Honduras.

1959    Cuban Revolution triumphs. Showdown with United States Missile crisis. Cuban alliance with Soviet Union in 1962. Cuba blockaded after 1964.

1960    Central American Economic Integration and Common Market Treaty. Costa Rica joins in 1963.

1960–1973    Guerrilla movement in Guatemala. Sandinista Front activities in Nicaragua.

1961    Kennedy formulates the Alliance for Progress.

1968–1982    Torrijos regime in Panama. Canal Treaty renegotiated in 1977.

1969    "Soccer War" between El Salvador and Honduras.

1971    Beginning of guerrilla movements in El Salvador.

1972–1978    "Military reformism" in Honduras.

1977    Guerrilla war revives in Guatemala; it centers in regions with majority Indian population.

1978–1979    Anti-Somoza struggle in Nicaragua. Sandinistas triumph in 1979.

1979–1980    Efforts at reform in El Salvador. The oligarchy fights back; Monsignor Romero assassinated in 1980.

1980    Economic crisis hits all Central American countries. Active U.S. presence in Honduras.

1981    Anti-Sandinista activities begin against Nicaragua with open support of the U.S.

1983    Diplomatic activities of the Contadora group begin with intent to pacify region. In October, the U.S. invades the Caribbean island of Grenada deposing a leftist regime allied with Cuba and Nicaragua.

1987    Peace Conference in Guatemala (Esquipulas II). President Arias's Peace Plan approved by the Central American governments.

# Notes

## 1. THE LAND AND THE PEOPLE

1. Being "Indian" is defined in purely cultural terms: language, dress, living in an Indian community, etc. Already by the eighteenth century, owing to the mixing of races, identification by purely phenotypic traits was difficult if not impossible.

## 2. THE COLONIAL PAST

1. "Tiene más de trezientos vezinos, y aquí ay mucha contratación de rropa y cacao."
2. Translator's Note: A "mark" (marco) is approximately 8 ounces or 230 grams.
3. Thomas Gage, *Travels in the New World*, edited and with an introduction by J. Eric. S. Thompson (Norman: University of Oklahoma Press, 1969).

## 3. IN SEARCH OF PROGRESS

1. Translator's Note: An area of measure in this region equal to about 33.3 acres.

## 6. THE PRESENT CRISIS

1. The following remarks are based on figures from CEPAL up to 1983 and on those provided by Victor Bulmer-Thomas, in "Cuentas Nacionales de Centroamérica desde 1920: Fuentes y métodos," *Anuario de Estudios Centroamericanos*, Universidad de Costa Rica, 12 (1), (1986): 81–96.
2. David Browning, "Agrarian Reform in El Salvador," *Journal of Latin American Studies* 1983, 15: 399–426.

## EPILOGUE

1. Dispatch 57, February 5, 1932, McCafferty to Secretary of State, General Conditions Report, January 1–31, 1932, p. 13. (Amer-

ican Legation: San Salvador, Correspondence, 1932, vol. III, File 800—in the National Archives, Washington, D.C.).

2. George F. Kennan, *Memoirs: 1925–1950* (Boston: Little, Brown and Company [An Atlantic Monthly Press Book], 1967), p. 322.

3. *Ladino* refers to persons primarily brought up and educated in the Spanish language and culture.

# Sources and Bibliography

The following only mentions some of the many bibliographic sources. The selections, reflecting the author's own preferences, also provide some suggestions for those interested in going deeper into the issues dealt with in the book. Sources dealing with a specific issue or country have been chosen to clarify the subject from a general regional viewpoint.

## GENERAL WORKS

Ralph Lee Woodward, Jr.'s book *Central America: A Nation Divided* (New York: Oxford University Press, 1976) is the only up-to-date general history. It is vastly superior to Mario Rodríguez's *América Central* (Mexico: Editorial Diana, 1967). A summary of the region's economic history can be found in Ciro F. S. Cardoso and Héctor Pérez Brignoli's *Centroamérica y la economía occidental, 1520–1930* (San José: Editorial Universidad de Costa Rica [EDUCA], 1977). Edelberto Torres Rivas's *Interpretación del desarrollo social centroamericano* (San José: EDUCA, 1971) is written from the theoretical perspective of "sociology of dependence."

Among the major journals, we can mention: *Estudios Sociales Centroamericanos* (San José: Confederación Universitaria Centroamericana, 1971 on); *Anuario de Estudios Centroamericanos* (Universidad de Costa Rica, 1974 on); *Revista Conservadora del Pensamiento Centroamericano* (Managua, 1960–1972), later reorganized under the title of *Revista del Pensamiento Centroamericano*. Let us also mention the special issue of the *Journal of Latin American Studies*, November 1983 (London), dedicated to Central America.

## THE LAND AND THE PEOPLE

The physical, political, and cultural geography of Central America are well presented in Robert West and John Augelli's excellent *Middle America: Its Lands and Peoples*, 2d ed. (Englewood Cliffs, N.J.: Prentice-Hall, 1976. In addition, one may consult volume 1 of the *Handbook of Middle American Indians* (Austin: University of Texas Press, 1964). Eric Wolf, in his classic work *Pueblos y culturas de Mesoamérica* (Mexico: Ediciones Era, 1967), offers a still unsurpassed overview of Native American cultures both past and present; and even though he concentrates on Mexico, he also studies the cultures of the Mayan region.

Nineteenth-century travelers provide vivid vignettes of daily life, descriptions of the countryside, and many other varied interesting items. Among these John L. Stephens's *Incidentes de viaje en Centroamérica, Chiapas y Yucatán* (San José: EDUCA, 1971), in two volumes, stands out; the original edition was published in 1841 and contains some magnificent etchings based on the drawings of F. Catherwood.

There are several studies on the relations between the United States and Central America and the Caribbean, but Lester Langley's *The United States and the Caribbean, 1900–1970* (Athens: The University of Georgia Press, 1980) is excellent. An overall study along the same lines covering the period 1776 to 1900 still needs to be done.

There is also a lack of good overviews on the growth of literature, the arts, and culture. The *Diccionario de la literatura latinoamericana: América Central*, 2 vols. (Washington, D.C.: Union Panamericana, 1963) provides a good bibliographical background and is easy to use. Rafael Heliodoro Valle's *Historia de las ideas contemporáneas en Centroamérica* (Mexico: Fondo de Cultura Economica, 1960) is too outdated to be profitably used now. However, Sergio Ramírez Mercado's essay, "Balcanes y volcanes, aproximaciones al proceso cultural de Centroamérica" (Balkans and volcanos, approaches to the cultural process of Central America) contained in Edelberto

Torres and others' *Centroamérica hoy* (Mexico: Siglo XXI, 1975), offers some suggestive views.

## THE COLONIAL PAST

Vast erudition and a modern overview are provided by Murdo MacLeod's *Spanish Central America: A Socioeconomic History. 1520–1720* (Berkeley, Los Angeles, London: University of California Press, 1973); and Miles Wortman's *Government and Society in Central America, 1680–1840* (New York: Columbia University Press, 1982). *La Patria del Criollo: Ensayo de interpretación de la realidad colonial guatemalteca* (Guatemala: Editorial Universitaria, 1971) by Severo Martínez Peláez is a magnificent study of collective psychology. Ideology and social domination are woven together by the inheritors of the conquistadors to create a new criollo nation. In the light of these two threads, certain conceptual errors and many hasty generalizations pale. There are two articles published years ago but which are still irreplaceable. These are: Robert S. Smith's "Indigo Production and Trade in Colonial Guatemala" in *Hispanic American Historical Review* 39. (1959): 181–211; and Troy S. Floyd's "The Guatemala Merchants, the Government, and the Provincianos, 1750–1800" in *Hispanic American Historical Review* 41. (1965): 90–110. We can still include Linda Newson's study "Labor in the Colonial Mining Industry of Honduras" in *The Americas*, October 1982: 185–203; Christopher Lutz's magnificent monograph on the capital city of the Kingdom of Guatemala, *Historia sociodemográfica de Santiago de Guatemala, 1541–1773* (Guatemala: CIRMA, 1983); and the still-unpublished thesis by Juan Carlos Solórzano, "Population et systémes économiques au Guatemala, 1690–1810" (Paris: Ecole des Hautes Etudes en Sciences Sociales, 1981). Concerning Panama, the reader should consult Omar Jaén Suárez, *La Población del Istmo de Panamá* (Panama, 1978); and various studies by Alfredo Castillero Calvo, in particular his *Economía terciaria y sociedad, Panamá siglos XVI y XVII* (Panama, 1980). Also useful is Walter LaFeber's study *The Panama Canal: The Crisis in Historical Perspective* (New

York: Oxford University Press, 1978). Dealing with Belize, there recently appeared a fairly extensive bibliography worth mentioning by Nigel O. Bolland, *Belize: A New Nation in Central America* (Boulder and London: Westview Press, 1986); and Narda Dobson's *A History of Belize* (London: Longman Caribbean, 1973).

## IN SEARCH OF PROGRESS

The transformation of the Central American Federation within the context of British diplomacy is very well investigated in Mario Rodríguez's *Chatfield, Cónsul Británico en Centroamérica* (Tegucigalpa: Banco Central de Honduras, 1970). A more general brief overview is to be found in the same author's *América Central* (Mexico: Editorial Diana, 1967). Also Thomas L. Karnes's *Los fracasos de la Unión, Centroamérica: 1824–1960* (San José: ICAP, 1982); and Ralph Lee Woodward's already mentioned study can be consulted. To study the Carrera rebellion one must go to Hazel Ingersoll's unpublished thesis, *The War of the Mountain: A Study of Reactionary Peasant Insurgency in Guatemala, 1837–1873* (Washington, D.C.: George Washington University Press, 1972). The William Walker episode has spawned a vast literature, but the best study continues to be William O. Scroggs's *Filibusteros y financieros: La historia de William Walker y sus asociados* (Managua: Banco de América, 1974), whose first edition was in 1916; as well as Walker's own account in *La querra de Nicaragua* (San José: EDUCA, 1970), first published in 1860.

Liberalism has stimulated numerous studies. *El pensamiento liberal de Guatemala* (San José: EDUCA, 1977) by Jorge Mario García Laguardia reprints the basic documents preceded by a long introduction. Thomas Herrick, in his *Desarrollo económico y político de Guatemala durante el período de Justo Rufino Barrios (1871–1885)* (Guatemala: EDUCA, 1974), analyzes the reform period knowledgeably without being limited to the traditional approach of overly emphasizing political institutional aspects. One should also consult Julio C. Cambranes's *Aspectos del desarrollo económico y social de Gua-*

*temala, a la luz de fuentes históricas alemanas, 1868–1885* (Guatemala: Universidad de San Carlos, Instituto de Investigaciones Económica y Sociales, 1975). *Oro de Honduras*, 2 vols. (Tegucigalpa, 1948–1954), an anthology edited by Rafael Heliodoro Valle, collects the major works of Ramáon Rosa, a noted Honduran Liberal who had a major influence in Central America. An eyewitness account, filled with irony and insight, of the turbulent and frequently contradictory politics of the period is to be found in the Nicaraguan writer Enrique Guzmán Selva's (1843–1911) *Diario Intimo*, which was published serially in the journal *Revista Conservadora del Pensamiento Centroamericano* (Managua) during the 1960s. Rafael Arévalo Martínez's *Ecce Pericles*, 2d ed. (San José: EDUCA, 1983), offers a passionate narrative chronicle of the Estrada Cabrera dictatorship. It is useful to read it in conjuction with Miguel Asturias's classic novel on the same theme, *El Señor Presidente*.

## IMPOVERISHING GROWTH

Among the various studies on the coffee economy, several stand out: David Browning's *El Salvador: La Tierra y el Hombre* (San Salvador: Ministerio de Educación, 1975); and Carolyn Hall's *El Café y el desarrollo histórico-geográfico de Costa Rica* (San José: Editorial Costa Rica, 1976). Both have the virtue of placing the problem within a broad historical and geographical context. Browning's work, in reality, reconstructs the changes in the countryside from the colonial period up to the present time. More limited is Sanford Mosk's essay "La economía cafetalera de Guatemala durante el período 1850–1918: su desarrollo y signos de inestabilidad" contained in the collection *Economía de Guatemala* (Guatemala: Seminario de Integración Social Guatemalteca, 1958). To study the banana plantations, Kepner and Soothill's *El imperio del banano* (Buenos Aires: Editorial Triángulo, 1957), of which there have been several editions, is still essential. It was first published in English in 1935. Novels by the Costa Rican author Carlos Luis Fallas, *Mamita Yunai*, and the Honduran writer Ramón Amaya Amador, *Prisión Verde*, vividly portray the life, struggle, and suffering on the plantations.

For Sandino there is a copious bibliography. There are several that merit particular mention: Neil Macauley's *The Sandino Affair* (Chicago: Quadrangle Books, 1967); and Sergio Ramírez Mercado's compilation of documents in *El Pensamiento Vivo de Sandino* (San Jose: EDUCA, 1974). Besides Langley's already mentioned study on U.S. policy and intervention, Dana G. Munro's various works are indispensable; in particular, *The United States and the Caribbean Republics, 1921–1933* (Princeton: Princeton University Press, 1974). The 1932 uprising in El Salvador has been studied by Thomas Anderson in *El Salvador, 1932*, 2d ed. (San José: EDUCA, 1982).

Covering unionizing struggles, there are two contemporary accounts of inestimable value. Roque Dalton's *Miguel Mármol: Los sucesos de 1932 en El Salvador* (San José: EDUCA, 1972); and Antonio Obando Sánchez's *Memorias, la historia del movimiento obrero en Guatemala en este siglo* (Guatemala: Editorial Universitaria, 1978).

## GROWING INEQUALITY

Guatemala's case has been particularly well studied. Richard Adams et al., *Crucifixion by Power: Essays on Guatemalan National Social Structure, 1944–1966* (Austin and London: University of Texas Press, 1970); and Robert Wasserstrom's "Revolución en Guatemala: Campesinos y políticos durante el gobierno de Arbenz" in *Estudios Sociales Centroamericanos*, Sept.–Dec. 1977 (San José) are both solid efforts to clarify the social structure and dynamics of political conflict. The 1954 U.S. intervention is examined by Susana Jonas Bodenheimer in her *Guatemala: Plan piloto para el continente* (San José: EDUCA, 1981) in terms of counterinsurgency strategies. Richard Immerman's *The CIA in Guatemala: The Foreign Policy of Intervention* (Austin: University of Texas Press, 1982); and Stephen Schlesinger and Stephen Kinzer's *Bitter Fruit: The Untold Story of the American Coup in Guatemala* (New York:

Anchor Books, 1983) make extensive use of classified State Department and CIA documents. They lay out in copious detail the planning and execution of the operation, clearly establishing its implications and the responsibilities. The Arbenz government's position is well put forth in Guillermo Toriello's *La Batalla de Guatemala* (Mexico: Cuadernos Americanos, 1955).

Regarding Costa Rica, John Patrick Bell's *Guerra civil en Costa Rica: Los sucesos políticos de 1984* (San José: EDUCA, 1976); and José Luis Vega Carballo's *Poder político y democracia en Costa Rica* (San José: Editorial Porvenir, 1982) can be consulted. The ups and downs of reform have been studied by Jorge Rovira Mas in his *Estado y política económica en Costa Rica, 1948–1970* (San José: Editorial Porvenir, 1982).

Richard Millet examines in detail the Somoza regime, focusing on the Nicaraguan National Guard in his *Guardianes de la dinastía* (San José: EDUCA, 1979), A broader historical perspective is taken by Alberto Lanuza et al. in their *Economía y sociedad en la construcción del Estado en Nicaragua* (San José: ICAP, 1983). On Honduras, there is Mario Posas and Rafael del Cit's *La construcción del sector público y del Estado Nacional en Honduras, 1876–1979* (San José: EDUCA-ICAP, 1981). *La guerra inútil: Análisis socioeconómico del conflicto entre Honduras y El Salvador* (San José: EDUCA, 1971), edited by Marco Virgilio Carias and Daniel Slutzky, goes well beyond the scope of the armed conflict of 1969. Concerning the utilization of resources, there is the excellent monograph by William H. Durham on Honduras and El Salvador, *Scarcity and Survival in Central America: Ecological Origins of the Soccer War* (Stanford: Stanford University Press, 1979). An even broader view, focusing on Costa Rica, is found in Carolyn Hall's important work, *Costa Rica: Una interpretación geográfica con perspectiva histórica* (San José: Editorial Costa Rica, 1984; English ed. by Westview Press, 1985).

The broadest study on industrialization and the Common Market (*Mercomún*) is the book edited by W. R. Cline and E. Delgado, *Economic Integration in Central America* (Washington, D.C.: The Brookings Institution, 1978). Changes in the banana economy have been magnificently studied by Frank Ellis in *Las transnacionales del banano en Centroamérica* (San José: EDUCA, 1983).

## THE PRESENT CRISIS

There is a vast bibliography dealing with U.S. policy, from which we can mention Walter Lafeber's *Inevitable Revolutions: The United States in Central America* (New York: Norton, 1983); and Richard Alan White's *The Morass: United States Intervention in Central America* (New York: Harper & Row, 1984).

Dealing with El Salvador, there is Enrique Baloyra's *El Salvador in Transition* (Chapel Hill: The University of North Carolina Press, 1982). It is absolutely vital to study Monsignor Romero's ideas. The anthology *Monseñor Romero* compiled by Arnoldo Mora (San José: EDUCA, 1981) unfortunately lacks an adequate index and fails to include certain important texts. Regarding agrarian reform, there is David Browning's article "Agrarian Reform in El Salvador," *Journal of Latin American Studies* 15 (November 1983).

The journal *Pensamiento propio* (Núm. 15, año II, Managua, 1984) has an interesting analysis on the five years of Sandinista government. There is also Michael E. Conroy's "False Polarization? Alternative Perspectives on the Economic Strategies of Post-Revolutionary Nicaragua" in *Third World Quarterly* (October 1984).

The violence in Guatemala is studied in detail by Gabriel Aguilera Peralta et al., in *Dialéctica del terror en Guatemala* (San José: EDUCA, 1981). One should also consult issue 10–11 of the journal *Polémica* (San José: ICADIS, July–October 1983); and issue 14–15 of *Polémica* (March–June 1984) has several retrospective articles on the Central American elections that took place during 1984.

## EPILOGUE: THE BURDENS OF THE PAST

The work of Las Casas is copious and abounds in references to Central America. His *Brevísima relación de la destrucción de las Indias* (1552) is the best known and most accessible; there have been numerous editions, one of which is the recent edition by André Saint-Lu (Madrid: Cátedra, 1984). Testimonies concerning torture, violence, and repression can be found in reports issued by Amnesty International, the Commission on Human Rights of the OAS, and the United Nations. A study that should not be omitted is Ricardo Falla's "Masacre de la finca San Francisco: Huehuetenango, Guatemala, 17 de julio de 1982" in *ECA, Revista de la Universidad Centroamericana Simeón Cañas* (San Salvador: July–August 1983), originally presented at the annual meeting of the American Anthropological Association in December of 1982.

The crime of Julian Tzul has been studied in Albertina Saravia Enriquez, *El ladino me jodió: vida de un indígena* (Guatemala, Editorial José Pineda Ibarra, 1983).

### BIBLIOGRAPHIES AND RESEARCH GUIDES

There are two large annotated bibliographies emphasizing materials available in English; they are found in the works of Ralph Lee Woodward and Lester Langley already referred to. For the scholar, the best guide is the recent work by Kenneth Grieb, *Research Guide to Central America and the Caribbean* (Madison: The University of Wisconsin Press, 1985).

# Index

Designer: U.C. Press Staff
Compositor: Auto-Graphics, Inc.
Text: 10/12 Palatino
Display: Palatino
Printer: Malloy Lithographing, Inc.
Binder: Malloy Lithographing, Inc.